A LAND FLOWING WITH MILK AND HONEY

A Land Flowing with Milk and Honey

PERSPECTIVES ON FEMINIST THEOLOGY

Elisabeth Moltmann-Wendel

SCM PRESS LTD

Translated by John Bowden from the German
Das Land, wo Milch und Honig fliesst,
published by Gütersloher Verlagshaus Gerd Mohn,
Gütersloh 1985.

British Library Cataloguing in Publication Data

Moltmann-Wendel, Elisabeth
A land flowing with milk and honey:
perspectives on feminist theology.
1. Christianity
I. Title II. Das Land wo Milch und Honig
fliesst. *English*
200   BR121.2

ISBN 0–334–00869–7

First British edition published 1986
by SCM Press Ltd
26-30 Tottenham Road, London N1

Phototypeset by Input Typesetting
and printed in Great Britain
by Richard Clay (The Chaucer Press) Ltd
Bungay, Suffolk

For Marjorie Casebier McCoy
Susanne Kahl-Passoth
Evi Krobath
Rosemarie Stappenbeck
Angelika Wagner

very different sisters

CONTENTS

List of Illustrations   xi

Introduction   1

Part One: Self-Discovery

1   Autonomy   13

    The image of women is changing   13
    Partnership   17
    Work   21
    Sexuality   23

2   What is Patriarchy?   29

    The experience of patriarchy   29
    Analyses of patriarchy   31
    Patriarchy and theology   36
    Male perspectives   38

3   The Forgotten Goddess   43

    Women's history   43
    Traces of women's cultures   48
    Women's societies   50
    The goddess today   53
    The results of research into matriarchy   56

Part Two: Critical Theology

4   Feminist Theology   63

    The model of liberation theology   63
    The experience of women   68
    Being a person   71
    Action and reflection   73

5   The Bible and Feminine Self-awareness   77

    The Bible and the women's movement   77
    The Jesus movement   79
    Patriarchal redaction   82
    Patriarchal reception   84
    Patriarchal interpretation and translation   87

6   God, our Mother   91

    Replacement of the Father   91
    The search for true mothers   93
    Wisdom   96
    Shekinah and Holy Spirit   98
    The non-patriarchal Father   99

7   Matriarchal Sub-culture   105

    The underside of history   105
    Unwritten traditions   107
    Woman and serpent   109
    The forgotten goddess in Christianity   111

Part Three: A New Perspective on the Stories about Jesus
    and Women

8   The Women's Jesus   117

    Feminist christology?   117
    The activity of women   121
    The senses   124
    Parallelism   127
    Excursus: The imperial Christ   133

9   Mutuality   137

    Women discover mutuality   137
    Positive and negative mutuality   138
    Disruption to the development of autonomy   141
    Male theology   143
    Dynamic relationship   145

CONTENTS

10 Self-love   151

   Justification and acceptance 151
   I am good 154
   I am whole 157
   I am beautiful 160

11 Patriarchal and Matriarchal Love   167

   The love of Sophia 167
   The patriarchy of love 170
   From God's love to love of God 172
   Loss of radical love 174
   The pedagogy of patriarchal love 177

12 Models for Women   181

   Trinities 181
   Anna Selbdritt 185
   The three women 188
   The pagan prehistory 191
   Mary and monolithic sisterhood 193
   Conclusion: The Bible and the Holy Spirit 197

Notes   203

LIST OF ILLUSTRATIONS

Mary Magdalene nominates Lazarus Bishop of Marseilles.   12
    Portable altar. Lübeck 1519, archive.

Pictorial representation of Spiritualism. Drawing, 1532.   28
    Clemens Ziegler, archive.

Cretan serpent goddess, around 1600 BC.   42
    Photo: Stephan Wehowsky

The crucified liberation.   62
    Painting by Gloria Guevara (Solentiname), archive.

The last communion of St Mary Magdalene in penitential
    dress.   76
    Tiefenbronn altar by Lucas Moser, 1431, archive.

Wisdom enthroned with seven books and a flowering
    sceptre.   90
    Eleventh-century Bible manuscript, Paris, archive.

Kether, Hokmuh and Binah – three feminine images of the
    Trinity.   104
    Didactic tablet of Princess Antonia, 1673, Bad Teinach,
        Urachhaus Verlag.

Albrecht Dürer, 'Christ on the Mount of Olives'.   116
    Pen drawing, 1521. Frankfurt, Städelsches Kunstinstitut.

Rembrandt, Christ healing Peter's mother-in-law, about 1659.   136
    Archive.

Eve, Rheims cathedral, about 1400.   150
    Archive.

Mediaeval devotional picture of St Anne.   166
    Altar in Niederlana. Hans Schnatterpeck, between 1503 and
        1510. Photo Frasnelli-Keitsch.

LIST OF ILLUSTRATIONS

The holy women at the tomb.   180
    Mozac cathedral, twelfth century. Edition du Lys.

INTRODUCTION

I

The land flowing with milk and honey is not a fool's paradise. It is not the ordinary person's dream of success, luxury, fleshpots and doing nothing. It is the dream of fertility and the natural order, a life based on natural resources – and it is the recollection of the standards of women's culture, for milk is the product of the mother and honey comes from bees governed by their queen. The qualities of life here are frugal and simple: natural, not concentrated food; matriarchal order, not patriarchy; a world of sufficiency in which good fortune is denoted by honey: it is good to be alive.

But the land of milk and honey has become a biblical heritage that we drag around with us thoughtlessly. Some suppose it to be a never-never land, a fool's paradise, and see milk as a sign of dependence on the mother, a pious way of thinking which gets in the way of rationality and maturity. Others say that it is a meaningless mythological formula, which simply contains dreams of unhistorical paradises.

However, it was with this vision of a land of milk and honey that the people of Israel went out of Egypt. Behind them lay slavery, but also the fleshpots of Egypt. God promised Moses 'a broad, free land, a land flowing with milk and honey', and this vision supported the people through the wilderness, through war, mortal danger and famine.

Because we do not suppose that the Jewish people set out from Egypt with an empty slogan, a crazy vision which could not be realized, we should think again about the image of milk and honey. Because we do not believe that the exodus, the break with old ties, which has motivated Judaism and Christianity in similar ways down to the present day, was bound up with an empty, unattractive promise, we should investigate the possible significance of the image. What was the attraction of milk and honey, that it proved stronger than the familiar fleshpots?

We are beginning to rediscover myths, and they communicate to us a basic human knowledge, a basic human experience. When we 'learn to read the myth' (Christa Wolf),[1] when we do not forget our rationality but let our reason mature in its wisdom, we sometimes come up against reminiscences, against other values and standards. Women in particular have experienced a 'horror at re-recognition' which has led them to interpret their existence and has prompted conceptions of another future.

In the cultures of the ancient Near East milk and honey are common images for the food of the gods, the food of paradise, the food of life. They were sacrificial gifts and were regarded as symbols of initiation right down to late antiquity. Milk, the first nourishment that comes from the mother, is here physical nourishment and in a transferred sense also spiritual nourishment. It gives both physical and spiritual life, both biological life and immortality. In many myths the hero, the king, is fed with it by the goddess, and it points to our origins of life and wholeness.

Religious studies and the psychology of religion suggest that the picture presented by the life of bees, from which honey comes, is 'the perfect example of the first human association based on the gynaecocracy of motherhood', in which the 'natural law is expressed more fully and with greater regularity than it is in human society'. In the 'Amazonian state of the bees', virginity, i.e. the relative lack of relations with the male, is striking; the queen bee is fertilized only once by the male, the other bees never. Demeter is regarded as the pure bee mother, and her bee priestesses must be virgins.[2]

For many people these are still conceptions of paradise without any real background, dream images of good old days which never were. But that is not true. We now know that there were probably no pure gynaecocracies (the rule of women), but that time and again there were cultures in which peace was possible, where there were few weapons, where aggression was limited and males and females had equal rights; where milk and honey flowed and were the priorities of life. But these images have been submerged by an aggressive culture where love of peace was banished, wars became 'necessary' and weapons important, and a cult of masculinity excluded women from playing a role in shaping society. The degree of power needed to obliterate such reminiscences of another life where the overcoming of grief and death which every society must achieve is not made even more difficult by human brutality is part of the history of human anxieties and aggression. Those who are on the way up, to domination and power, usually cut off their roots in a brutal way.

Psychologists of religion in search of humanity and images of human origin are again taking up this picture: according to Erich Fromm, milk is the symbol of the first aspect of love, care and reassurance. For him honey symbolizes,

> the sweetness of life, the love for it and the happiness in being alive. Most mothers are capable of giving 'milk', but only a minority of giving 'honey' too. In order to be able to give honey, a mother must not only be a 'good mother', but a happy person... The mother's love for life is as infectious as her anxiety is.[3]

Where belief in progress is becoming questionable and productivity and efficiency are no longer absolutes, where we are concerned with the psychological and ecological dimensions of the natural resources of human life, the land of milk and honey takes on new contours. Now Moses, the man of God, left Egypt in the company of the children of Israel with this dream of a non-patriarchal order of life. However, all those who attained self-awareness in the context of Jewish-Christian faith have missed almost all its subversive elements. The Jewish-Christian tradition is carried on by patriarchs and shaped by men who have taken little notice of the feminine element within themselves and outside themselves, and so to many women today it seems to be crudely patriarchal.

Still, the image of milk and honey remains deeply embedded

3

in it and permeates the Old Testament. Regardless of what ancient Near Eastern culture may have sponsored it, in the Israelite exodus a matristic myth of origins (i.e. one which comes from a women's culture) has been transformed into the goal of a wandering. Yet, as happens with all those who identify themselves with the patriarchal culture, this picture has conjured up no kind of associations with past value-systems, even among theologians. Old Testament scholars have wondered whether milk and honey might reflect the cultural stage of nomads or peasants. Milk and honey are regarded as an empty cliché for the natural fertility of Palestine[4] – even if the cliché occurs at least nineteen times in the Old Testament and should therefore attract more attention. It is thought to be 'worn out', a 'stereotyped formula' deriving from the ancient Near East, as an 'age-old combination of the choice gifts of nature', 'a recollection of a lost happiness and the hope of a modest recurrence'.[5]

The discrepancy from Israelite reality is, however, striking. In Israel milk has little significance, little symbolic content, and as a symbol at most stands for 'whiteness' and riches. Whereas in neighbouring cultures milk and honey were food of the gods, sacrificial gifts and symbols of initiation, Israel knew of no goddess who suckled the king, and therefore did not have milk as an initiation symbol. Instead of natural gifts, milk and honey, here human products, oil and grain and the Dionysian, male wine were offered. Milk, without which human origins and wholeness are inconceivable, was transferred to the masculine God: 'God gives suck' (Deut.32.13). 'God's loving breast gives us milk' (Clement of Alexandria). This old symbol was taken over by males and at the same time transformed; the myth of origin became an eschatological slogan for the journey which again pointed beyond the patriarchal Israelite culture. How do we deal with this contradiction?

II

For me the mythical image of milk and honey which stands at the beginning of the Jewish tradition is significant in three ways. First, it signifies a latent world of women within this tradition which –

as everywhere else – is hidden, invisible and never seen. Perhaps it shows elements of resistance against a rising masculine culture. It is ridiculed and discriminated against. However, perhaps also within its thought-patterns and institutions, despite its sub-cultural and possibly even subversive character, this remnant has preserved a criterion for humanity and human relationships. What Horst Eberhart Richter assumes to be the significance of women for a human society 'in the subordinate background position assigned to them', the damming up of the 'escapades of male arrogance which could end in universal destruction',[6] can also apply to religions. Where would a theology of liberation be without the Old Testament songs of liberation sung by Miriam, Judith and Deborah? What role did women play in all Christian oppositions between resistance and surrender? What bearing on reality shaped them and their decisions? What would a church bureaucracy be without, for example, the activity of women's groups? However, we can no longer be content with becoming aware of our background position. Still, it can be a basis on which we can represent the necessary continuity within the changes which take place in us and apply to us.

Many women today are asking whether Christianity is hope-lessly patriarchal. This corresponds with many experiences in life and literature from Paul via Augustine and Karl Barth to the Vatican Declaration on the Admission of Women to the Priest-hood. Despite such experiences and despite the oppressive docu-mentation, it seems to me that the level of reality for women evident from myths, which are often unconscious or read in a new light, a level of reality that is made clear by scholarship, has been overlooked. For me, the image of the land flowing with milk and honey expresses a reality for women within the Jewish-Christian tradition which is invisible and yet present, above all for those who see God on the side of the weak, the poor, women and those without rights, despite other oppressive experiences. God on the gallows, on the cross; God not as a male dream or a heroic epic. No Christ in the victor's pose. God where no church seeks him. God where women live and establish their values. Where God is also revered as woman, as mother, as wisdom.

Feminist theology is in search of this identity and history and of an independent future for women. It is concerned with the invisibility of women. But at the same time it is also concerned with the invisibility of a non-patriarchal God, and if that is at all possible, it seeks the disclosure of both and the use of them as criteria.

Secondly, what we encounter in the images of earlier cultures, what we learn to read in myth and what helps us to cope with the present, is matched by the insights of psychoanalysis and social therapy. One of its representatives, Jean Baker Miller, writes:

> Psychoanalysis, in attempting to probe the depth of the human psyche, entered the 'unreal world' of mankind's unsolved problems of mankind (= 'maleness'); in threading its way through the many complicated labyrinths, it did not recognize it for what it was: woman's world. What society has so far failed to see is that living contact with the unreal world need not make you weaken us. It can strengthen us all. [7]

In a male society with male standards for concepts, patterns of thought and conduct, language and values, women are diverted from their own reality. By becoming aware of themselves today, again trusting their experiences, no longer ridiculing them, they discover another reality and its values.

What does autonomy mean to them? The ideal of independence from relationships with men and their laws? Hardly that!

What does self-realization mean to them? Certainly not elbow room at the expense of others!

What is power? Hardly pushing things through blindly, but rather working, being effective in freedom.

In the light of their own values, women also have questions about dominant theories and theologies: the destructive image of humanity, its egoism, its disruptive structure of drives and the pedagogy and social theory which emerges from it. A society which is based on this 'can only hope to hold this destructiveness in check and to sublimate these drives' (Jean Baker Miller).

Similar things also happen in theology: the distorted image of humanity confronted with a good and perfect will of God can only lead to conflict: to the breaking of the will, the ethic of obedience and the rituals of a black pedagogy. Is there no accord with the will of God? Is there no other discipleship than that of obedience, 'our supreme and most noble contribution' (Adolf Schlatter)[8] – out of delight, out of self-love on the basis of love of the neighbour?

Being directed back towards another aspect of reality – and this is not exclusively the reality of women; it is also the mark of men who leave the old pattern of life – does not relieve us of conflict, of clashes with the other apparently real reality. This is not a game, and it takes generations. But the nucleus of reality in what emerges in us and in the history of humanity may help to stabilize us, to bring another reality to bear, to see the basis of the facts and yet not put down eternal roots there.

And there is yet a third element for me in the image of the land flowing with milk and honey. Here is the picture of a *land*, room for all to live in; it may be a mother symbol, but it is not a goddess image with which only women can identify. I want to begin with the question many women ask about their identity, but at the same time to go beyond it. For the question of female identity by itself all too often ends up in a rigid feminist principle and at the same time founders on reality as most women experience it. Many women see themselves on a journey in a feminist spirituality or religiousness supposing that they will get nearer to this feminist principle in the goddess, achieve it and celebrate it. They no longer see the offer of milk and honey, origin and identity, quality of life and happiness, in Christianity. But in departing from Christianity they soon get hooked on a self-centred, self-satisfied piety.

I want to extend the question of identity to the question of values, to the relationships which make up life and which take place between all human beings. What has not been done justice to in a patriarchal culture? What has been overlooked so that the human values and the original human relationships embodied in them have been pushed to the side? What values do women contribute which first go to make real humanity? What does the story of Jesus and his dealings with women contribute here as a real Christian paradigm?

These questions not only relate to women. They also concern men who perceive their narrowness and their anxieties. The land of milk and honey is not a mother country which will swallow them up, reduce them and make them dependent. It is an offer to experience anew our origins and our identity, our quality of life and our happiness, to redeem the notion of fathers whom they forgot in their haste at setting out, with excessive expectations, in male arrogance. It is an offer of a return to healing and a new orientation on the possibilities of peace and a just communal life. From here there opens up the whole breadth of a land with room for all to live in, which offers personal growth along with bread and wine and meat.

The question of identity which concerns women at present is therefore not the last question they ask. 'The habit of freedom and the courage to write exactly what we think' (Virginia Woolf) has still to be achieved. Whatever eschatological or future hope women have is varied and hardly of general validity. Virginia Woolf gave women a lead, 'that we go alone and that our relation is to the world of reality and not only to the world of men and women.' Real life is communal life and not the 'little separated lives which we live as individuals'.[9]

This seems to me to describe what in Christian terminology we call the eschaton. That is not merely a remote condition; it also already determines our present. For us who so urgently and definitively seek our identity it may be like self-forgetfulness, 'the courage to write exactly what we think'. Sometimes it already overtakes us and is not against us. It rounds out and completes our selfhood.

III

From these aspects of the history of culture and social psychology which seem to me best to reproduce the reality and the existential interests of women, I want to offer some perspectives on feminist theology.

Women's reality of women and women's interests are very broad conceptions. But they best denote the vitality and search for self-determination among women in different spheres which are documented in pictures, symbols, forms of rebellion and alternative forms of life and are even now visibly present. My hermeneutical starting point is a concept of autonomy derived from counselling women, which can also be significant for men today. It does not denote a rationalistic, individualistic self-determination, but self-determination within a context of relationships. To take as a hermeneutical starting point perspectives drawn from the present, e.g. power and sexuality, seems to me to narrow the approach since such perspectives *a priori* imply sacrifice and powerlessness.

One trend in feminist theology, that of seeing Christianity in terms of the history of its negative effect on women and as being hopelessly patriarchal, seems to me to be too facile. However, it would also be fatal to close one's eyes to its numerous political errors and theological distortions and to the claim which is still put forward today that men are its only legitimate representatives. I am concerned not to demonize Christianity in its many forms nor to make theology neurotic, but to trace origins and distortions, to bring them to the level of consciousness, to make them visible and capable of being transcended.

For many women today traditional theology is a phantom of which they would really like to be rid. Feminist theology is therefore also above all a grass-roots movement of an experimental kind, with emphases in the arts, therapy and politics. I myself have always found in traditional theology islands of freedom and selfhood, authentic forms of expression and social motivation. Encouragement and suggestions for this book therefore also came above all from the USA, where women's theology has entered into a creative conversation with traditional theology and its thought-patterns.

So after dealing in the first part with questions of feminine self-discovery which seem to me to be important, and in the light of that in the second part dealing critically with the findings of traditional theology, in the third part I want to begin from centres of Reformation theology which have still continued to remain alive for me: christology and the doctrine of justification. I have retitled them 'The Women's Jesus' and 'Self-love'. From there I want to attempt a reorientation of feminist theology. Anyone who wants to learn something new about feminist theology should begin at that point. In particular in the stories about Jesus' relationships with women, I see in the New Testament and experience in my work with women from very different backgrounds a story and an experience of women which is still far from being exhausted and which can provide new models by which both women and men can think and live. Here I join company with my earlier book, *The Women around Jesus*, and reflect in more marked theological terms on its approach. However, the present book is not addressed to an academic public, although it contains research and has notes to enable further research. It is addressed to lay women and women theologians, to lay men and men theologians, to all who are interested in new thought and thus in becoming aware of themselves.

Chapters 1.2; 2.2; 2.3 were written in connection with the special project on 'Women and Christianity' financed by the Volkswagen Foundation at the Institute for Ecumenical Research (headed by Professor Dr Hans Küng) in the University of Tübingen.

I would like to thank here all those who followed the manuscript critically and creatively in its final phases, with patience and skill, and whose contributions gave me more suggestions than I could take up in the book: Dr Christine Janowski, Evi Krobath, Professor Dr Angelica Wagner, Dr Stephan Wehowsky and my husband. I would also like to thank Dr Wilhelm von Braunmühl, who looked after the proofs skilfully and with commitment.

Tübingen,   Elisabeth Moltmann-Wendel
October 1984

Part One: Self-Discovery

Mary Magdalene nominates Lazarus Bishop of Marseilles.
Portable altar. Lübeck 1519

1

AUTONOMY

Only learning – or relearning – feminine, i.e. human autonomy
can save the planet from becoming uninhabitable.

Irmtraud Morgner

The image of women is changing

The changed way in which women understand themselves is
fundamental to feminist theology. It has many causes and
many effects. Even if no two women are alike and every
woman goes her own way, we can establish trends and parallels
which have developed over recent years. The old bourgeois
Christian view of women, giving them separate functions, that
appeared in 1963 in the *Lexikon für Theologie und Kirche*,
gives us a starting point:

> She (the woman) is a different but equal consort of the man
> in marriage, the heart of the family and mother of children.
> Therefore in the state... the woman appropriately represents
> the female side of culture, maternal love in all spheres...
> Through the advance of liberalist and Marxist ideologies
> the woman has increasingly made progress in professional
> work... through a mechanical and false understanding of
> equal rights the essentially loving attitude of the woman has
> often been distorted into a struggle for recognition which in
> fact threatens to prove the end of her characteristic power...
> (article 'Frau').

There are many causes of this change which has taken place
over the last twenty years.
1. A growing democratization of our society as a conse-

quence of which the equal status of women laid down as a fundamental right is being put into practice in various spheres. Women are becoming aware of their rights and possibilities in their places of work and in the family.

2. Developments in medical research, e.g. the invention of the pill, which primarily gives women an opportunity to have more control over their own bodies.

3. An increasing individualization and pluralization in our culture and society, a breakdown in conceptions of order which bring an awareness of the loss of the wider family and raise the question of the identity of the individual.

4. The minority movement throughout the world, which has embraced coloured people, youth, the disabled and also women, and which calls them to self-determination and taking responsibility for themselves.

5. The contemporary women's movement, feminism, which contains many of the trends mentioned above, but in particular seeks to analyse and change the psychological, social, economic and cultural situation of women.

This last point is the decisive one, but for many people it is also the most difficult; the word feminism arouses anxiety among men and also among many women: anxiety about aggression and regression, the seizing of power by women. But no one who is seriously concerned with the situation of women in our culture can avoid the feminist challenge with its acute analyses.

I want here to go briefly into the origin of the movement and its central concern. Whereas the earlier women's movement at the turn of the century was concerned with equal rights for women and their integration into a patriarchal society, the new movement is concerned with the self-determination of women and the changing of values in a patriarchal society. Many women who played an active role in the 1968 student movement against a capitalist exploitation of the workers are now discovering in the power of the state to control their bodies, in the prohibition of abortion or the termination of pregnancy, an even deeper-seated social evil, sexism (the oppression of one sex by the other), which in fact antedated capitalism. The corporeality and sexuality of women was discovered to be the central area of experience from which personality is formed. It was no longer to be constricted by the demands of childbearing or exploited in economic terms. This gave rise to surprising new aspects first for the woman herself, her historical, present and future role, and secondly for the deforming structure of our patriarchal society. Women discovered that they were victims of a policy which is grounded in the superiority of the male and his sexual domination. They discovered that as a consequence of this, motherhood remained their real destiny and calling and that this would involve marriage and the existence of a housewife. They saw themselves as victims of a many-sided oppression which extends from brute physical force through psychological oppression to political impotence. Some may be shocked at the tone of these charges, but the wounds of our society in which women lay their fingers are now visible to all. Here I would simply recall the homes for women which over recent years have mushroomed all over our country, the need for which no local politician doubts.

The other important aspect of the feminist challenge was that the deforming structure of the patriarchy became clear not only to women but also to men, and came to involve psychologists, doctors and sociologists. The old patriarchal ordering of the world according to which the man takes possession of reason and will and woman is left only with the heart was seen to divide both person and society and to be the cause of illnesses and diseases. The control of the woman by the man – as now became clear – is matched by the control of the will and the understanding over our body, which defends itself against this domination by sickness. (The exploitation of nature is to be seen as a parallel to this!) Guido Groeger has observed how, in convalescent homes for mothers, women today are asking questions about emancipation in the form of psychosomatic illnesses. They have psychosomatic illnesses to the point of being devoured by cancer because burdens are too great, possibilities of development and growth are destroyed or cramped, or because people have too little time for them, for love and tenderness.

No matter which of these various influences – equal rights, medical technology, cultural individuation and so on – has gained the upper hand, women's eyes are being opened to a new world which for many of them has proved liberating, but has terrified many others. By no means all women are capable of the autonomy which they now need to form opinions and develop awareness. A new feminist literature overwhelms them with a wealth of new insights and hypotheses: that e.g. they do not come into the world as 'women' but become women; that they look on their male babies differently from their daughters and bring them up more freely.

On the other hand they are led on e.g. by the publicity for the beautiful clean world of the housewife and mother who is consumed with love for her family – a picture which is easy to accept because it hands on the sacrifical role that they have learned and does not produce the risk of any loss of love on the part of the family.

Brought up by mothers and kept in a close symbiotic relationship to them, as the mothers themselves were dependent and often immature, women find it much more difficult than men to become autonomous, mature and independent. Brought up to self-control instead of self-love and made deeply uncertain by it, women have not learnt to ask about themselves, their wishes, aims and needs to the degree that men have. The offer to come to terms with their own past often terrifies them. Views which come from the field of radical feminism also evoke anxiety about supposed misandry and prevent them working through their sense of dependence. Female 'misandry' threatens their own existence, aware as they are that they are never completely independent of the male but cannot free themselves completely from their mothers either, and therefore live in anxiety and dependence. On the other hand, the death of a partner or divorce forces women to an independence which evidently they never wanted. Some manage to make a full life of their own – it is amazing how many gifts they have. But between the experience of female socialization and the compulsion or wish to become themselves there is a gap which for many people is difficult to close. The quest for autonomy has begun. But it is an autonomy which needs a new version specifically for women.

I want to demonstrate from three spheres of existence, partnership, work and sexuality, what it means today for women to develop their own autonomy, to work out female socialization and to take independent steps into new territory.

Partnership

The traditional feminine sphere is marriage and partnership. However, a generation of younger women in particular regards the sense of finding identity only in partnership as a relic of patriarchal dependence which they want to abolish. They think that partnership is the 'sleeping pill of emancipation', which hinders self-development and autonomy.

Anxiety about ties, anxiety about losing oneself in such ties, anxiety about mothers, the primal models of such ties, drives many of them today to achieve autonomy and personality in their work. If they do enter into a relationship and then break it off again, the majority of them are the active ones who initiate the break.

However, the experience of many women hitherto has been that partnership with another person is part of their identity. In studies in the psychology of women's development Carol Gilligan has established that the concept of identity 'expands to include the experience of interconnection'. Some contemporary demands for autonomy as the only way in which the individual achieves self-determination and self-realization by the establishment of personal interests therefore seem to them

17

to be alien to reality, irreconcilable with their own reality and a threat to it. Women, as the psychotherapist Jean Baker Miller confirms,

> stay with, build on and develop in a context of attachment and affiliation with others. Indeed, women's sense of self becomes very much organized around being able to make and then to maintain affiliations and relationships. Eventually, for many women, the threat of disruption of an affiliation is perceived not as just a loss of relationship but as something closer to a total loss of self.[1]

As much research has shown, this psychological structure may have been inculcated, in that the mother has refused the small daughter autonomy longer than the small son. It may also have a biological background in that girls use the two halves of the brain, the emotional and the rational, differently from boys. There are signs that in girls a perception of forms runs through both hemispheres, and that they have a stronger capacity for the integration of the rational and the emotional aspects of life, which probably has consequences for other spheres of life.[2] (Be this as it may, I am not referring here to the biological difference between the sexes on which society and theology have been built up for centuries and which has been caricatured to the point of talking in terms of the 'physiological weakmindedness of the woman'.)

This experience of finding fulfilment only in partnership is increasingly comng into conflict with the reality of life for many women in present society: their work calls for a capacity to impose themselves, while bringing up children calls for a readiness to become detached from them. The isolation of old age is more strongly felt by women than by men, for whom women love to cook and care. The present reality of a woman's life calls to a greater degree than before for her to develop her self and learn autonomy.

Women are more exposed, more vulnerable – vulnerable, too, in economic terms – and affected more deeply in their sense of self-esteem than men when partnerships break up. The complaint of the African woman Mariama Bâ shows that this also applies to marriages in patriarchal societies outside the European cultural area:

> I am trying to recognize my guilt in the failure of my marriage. I have given without calculating, given more than I got back. I am one of those who can only realize myself and develop in life with a partner. I have never understood the happiness in a life without a partner, even if I respected the choice of free women. I loved my home. You can see that I made it a place of peace, where everything had its place and a harmonious symphony of colours prevailed. You know my sensitivity, the boundless love that I felt for Modou. You can bear witness that I was on my feet day and night in his service and read every wish from his lips... And my children grew up without telling lies. Their success in school was all my pride, so to speak my laurel, which I laid at the feet of my lord.[3]

This typical conflict in marriage which is particularly tragic by virtue of the sacrifices of the woman partner for it, shows that the problem lies less in the relationship of the partners than in our traditional form of marriage and family which makes it difficult for the woman to discover herself (and also gives the survivor the feeling of 'not being a complete person'). For centuries marriage and family, procreation and house-keeping were the only spheres in which the woman could develop and find confirmation of her capacities for integration. In a society which is dividing increasingly markedly into private and public spheres, it has become more and more difficult for women to find public recognition and confirmation of these activities. In contemporary traditional marriage with its divisions of function, to which is added the present pressure to achieve status exercised by the community – the extra-large living room is a sign of this – the development of autonomy and individuality becomes particularly difficult. The capacities of the woman are absorbed by the family without her receiving public recognition. At present the basic need to find identity and partnership and at the same time to develop autonomy creates a conflict which it is almost impossible to resolve. The 'problem without a name' to which in 1963 Betty Friedan applied the term 'feminine delusion' she now sees as the problem of how women can combine job, love, home and children without losing themselves.[4]

In many situations children offer wives substitute solutions for a lack of identification with the husband. But the children increasingly resist that role and painfully challenge women to find their own selves. Bringing up children is still a kind of self-surrender which in phases demands identification with them, their needs and the rhythm of their lives. It is then a balancing act: not being the eternal nanny of the children, developing a life of one's own, giving oneself to them and yet letting go at the decisive moment.

However, we must again learn to see something of self-realization in a successful process of detachment: 'When they (the children) held each other's hands,' wrote a woman lecturer from East Germany, 'I had the comforting feeling that the meaning of my life was fulfilled. I had realized myself in my children.'[5] This development, which so many women find so negative, which fills them with anxiety and a sense of abandonment, is in the long run possible only if they also find fulfilment outside the family, and if ties to children, to the husband, to the partner, are no longer felt to be merely dependence but are regarded as an extension and fulfilment of their human possibilities which has already been voluntarily and consciously entered into.

The question is how women can return to trust and to ties without damaging themselves or hating themselves, and how in so doing they can remain themselves. The basic presupposition for this is that 'it can meet up with the idea that first and above all they are there for the well-being and fulfilment of the wishes and needs of the others' (Jean Baker Miller). Only then can they begin to get to know themselves.

Work

The first woman in Germany to speak in public at a church gathering, the Protestant Social Congress, was Elisabeth Gnauck-Kühne. In 1895 she said to the men assembled there: 'Gentlemen, whatever personal disaster may befall you, your work is the firm framework within which your life moves. It gives it internal equilibrium.'[6] This experience is still confirmed today. To begin with, in fact work seems a less problematical field in which a woman can become herself. Most recent investigations among female factory workers show that 'pride in the product' even outweighs the pressures of children and home and contributes towards the formation of personality. Her work gives the woman economic independence, which is a stabilizing factor contributing towards a feeling of wholeness. Further, it provides a feeling of social worth which cannot be had in the same way in and through the family. Sociological investigations constantly show how this feeling of social worth extends beyond economic necessity or the wish to have more money. From the report of the 1980 commission of enquiry in West Germany it emerges that the number of working women among the female population of West Germany has hardly changed since 1950. However, the awareness of women has changed. In 1968 only twenty-seven per cent of women workers were in favour of a married woman taking on other work in addition to her home and job. By 1975 this had already reached seventy-five per cent.

Many women want to understand themselves in terms of their job. However, this is not a reality for all of them. The reality is that unemployment among women is rising, that part-time employment is hard to find, and that the woman is the only one in our society who is expected to look after the children.

However, to see housekeeping and motherhood as a lifelong profession has its perils and the house-husbands who are appearing today all over the place openly concede that they envisage themselves engaging in this activity only for a limited time.

A Berlin housewife describes how difficult it is to combine a feeling of self-importance which arises from achievement with family work:

It's just the small details which make me mad. My husband never takes the empty beer can back to the kitchen and I keep having to say to the children 'Do this, Do that'. Whatever I do is undone again in a moment. What I cook gets eaten with moans, what I wash gets dirty, what I tidy up gets muddled, what I clean gets dirty again... I find it easier to love people with whom I don't live together so closely...[7]

In the long run it is hard for a feeling of self-esteem to develop in this sphere which is a mixture of work and love. Objective activities of their own, some of them outside the house, forming an extension of the subjective sphere of family work, give women continuity. Most women find that even honorary activities which call for other modes of behaviour make them more balanced, stable and mature. To expect all women to have a job in which they develop autonomy would be illusory today. But it is not illusory to expect families to have courage for flexibility, for an exchange of roles, or to stimulate the imagination of women to discover activities outside the house.

Something else is important: jobs or activities outside the house give women the possibility of taking part in social progress and attempting to bring about changes. Here, however, they will find the smallest beginnings and the greatest disappointments. Increasing unemployment and the retreat of women from important spheres produces resignation among many women. That often means a withdrawal into the private sphere and thus a loss of autonomy, social experience and responsibilites. In key positions women are in a minority and are always in danger of adapting themselves to traditional society and its laws. It is more utopia than reality to expect women to introduce into society the integrative capacities which are distinctive of them.

Sexuality

The sphere in which a woman's experience of herself is still least articulated is that of sexuality. So far, too few women have been able to develop a stable feeling of self, so that in this tabu sphere tradition-bound, deeply-rooted values and attitudes change only slowly. People do not talk much about sexuality, least of all women, and the theory of penis-envy which has been popularized in the context of Freud's all-prevalent psychoanalysis has been another factor in making women uncertain and trapping them within the limitations of patriarchal prejudices.

But it is precisely in the sphere of sexuality that many women see the real centre of their experience of themselves, which had been suppressed, violated and delivered over to male practices. In the women's movement women speak with striking openness about their bodies and their sexual desires. They have learned self-exploration as a way of discovering their own bodies and rediscovered the clitoris as the real focus of a woman's pleasure. War has been declared on all stereotyped role models of sexuality in which women have been given a special place as sex object, sacrifice, vamp. At the same time the male domination which has been behind this was fought and brought to consciousness: that male domination which repeats its idea of performance in coitus at the expense of the woman, which wants penetration rather than tenderness. Males have also been discovered to have been educated wrongly and to act wrongly in the sphere of sexuality: in place of this there has been encouragement towards a cheering, undemanding tenderness which meets the needs of the other and can be bisexual.

However, there was and still is the greatest difficulty for women to emerge from their old attitude, which for many of them is a passive one. As Margarete Mitscherlich points out, 'The woman's anxiety and shame about her sexuality are associated above all with sexual excitement which is introduced and experienced on her own initiative. Most women feel that sexuality should only be aroused by the male.'[8] Female sexuality is still a dark continent, a land of discovery for the woman – and also for the man. Women from Christian traditions with the fixed, traditional sexuality of the church on their backs have found it most difficult to follow here. On the other hand the constant complaint of the women's movement about the violation of the woman in many spheres has in the long run proved more of a deterrent than an encouragement and has cemented the passive role of women. Marlis Gerhardt indicates the consequences: 'In the last resort the description of an extreme act of physical violence helps to portray a woman as a sacrifice, conjuring up the old picture of feminine humiliation and hurt.'[9] This 'neuroticizing of daily relationships' between human beings – as the doyenne of the American women's movement, Betty Friedan, now sees it – cripples and dulls the experience and the constant communication of mutilation, but does not produce any new relationships. The white spaces on the feminist map stand out particularly sharply here. It is a problem for many women today to become aware of the oppression and violation that does take place (rape in marriage is not a punishable crime) and nevertheless show ways to new relationships.

Marina Möller-Gambaroff sees the possibility of an 'autonomous sexuality' in a 'non-repressive sexuality' in which both partners take both active and passive roles.[10] Here the roles of 'subject' and 'object' are not fixed, but regularly interchangable and pleasurable in themselves. However, this presupposes a radical investigation of one's own needs and the anxieties associated with them: in the case of the woman anxiety over activity, in that of the man anxiety more over impotence and passivity.

At all events, for many women today there is a new openness in speaking about what happens in their bodies. Sexuality is not a matter of performance, and this experience is also extending to men and freeing them from the compulsion they have acquired always to have to be potent. A newly discovered sphere of tenderness, freedom for a culture of contact, kissing, embracing, has come into being and creates new happy relationships and feelings of pleasure beyond the old sexual roles with their pressures towards performance.

The many facets of female sexuality, 'the geography of her pleasure' (Luce Irigaray), extend beyond physical contact into spheres which hitherto we have hardly come to associate with sexuality and in which powers can be evoked which will affect imagination, thought, language and thus plans for the self and the question of God. The constriction of thought among women as a result of sexual oppression which was already noted by Freud also prevents them from standing by their own ideas of value and morality.

Here autonomy can and must develop. This is a centre from which social impetus can come. What do women want today? Ten years ago Dorothee Sölle's answer was, 'We do not want to become like the men in our society, crippled beings emotionally impoverished under the pressure of having to achieve.' This negative definition has now increasingly been replaced by a personal feeling which Helke Sanders puts like this:

Standing on our own feet,
seeing with both eyes
and feeling pleasure.[11]

There may be discussion as to whether we are born as women or brought up to be women. But that is almost a secondary, academic question. The aim women cherish and which they often experience among themselves is a more human society, and in a culture where the male is caught up in competition and the need to achieve they are already showing that people need both dimensions – autonomy and society, achievement and tenderness – in order to become completely whole.

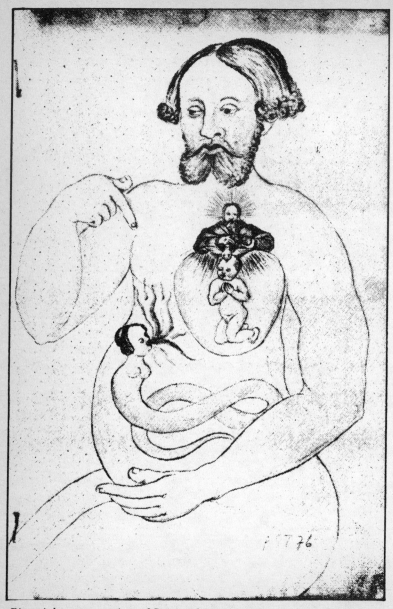

Pictorial representation of Spiritualism, which is classed with the 'radical' Reformation: in the body evil is fighting against the seat of the soul in the heart (drawing by Clemens Ziegler, 1532)

2

WHAT IS PATRIARCHY?

A man can be destroyed but not defeated.

Ernest Hemingway

The experience of patriarchy

At the present time the word 'patriarchy' (patriarchal) has many dimensions which we shall now investigate more closely. On the one hand 'patriarchy' has become a slogan to which many women resort in their attack on the intolerable domination of men. The result of this is to induce anxiety and antipathy to the word among those who feel threatened by it or who feel that it represents an attack on existing values and orders. On the other hand 'patriarchy' has become a handy notion which reproduces psychological and social conditions and which can be used in arguments.

As this concept has not just developed in the course of new theorizing but has above all arisen from a changed basic structure of female consciousness, I would first of all like to begin with characteristics and experiences of everyday patriarchy in which we are often unconsciously involved.

1. Wives are defined in terms of their husband: Mrs Smith, the pastor's wife and so on. An engineer whose wife is a woman minister is hardly likely to be called the minister's husband. Women become identified with their husband's profession and his role in society and find it increasingly difficult to find their own identity. The husband determines the social status and the activity of the wife. She accompanies him in 'emotional self-surrender'. She still has her heart, but to offer it is a

'service that may be called on at any time' (Horst Eberhard Richter).

2. In our traditional understanding of ourselves the man is the one with reason and will. He determines what nature is. The sexuality and corporeality of the wife are subject to his intellectual, moral, physical and psychological domination. According to Freud's theory of penis-envy the wife has no sexuality of her own. Nietzsche's statement, 'The husband's happiness is called "I want" and the wife's happiness is called "He wants"', still applies to the dominant understanding of the sexes. This domination of the female sex is at the same time a domination of the female attributes which men also have. So the *anima* of the husband, his own world of feelings, also suffers from this domination and oppression (see the plate on p.28). If a person is brought up only to repression and self-control, something of that wholeness which belongs to every person, including the male, suffers.

3. Women draw their self-confidence and feelings about themselves from mothers who have internalized this non-identity by traditional structures and who because they have an inadequate sense of self and are not guided by views of their own cannot let go of their daughters, thus forcing them into the same inferior role. By contrast sons do not have to fulfil the unfulfilled expectations of their mothers and this on the one hand gives them greater freedom and self-confidence and on the other drives them towards self-assertion through achievement. In an investigation of the relationship of mothers to the generation of new women, Marina Möller-Gambaroff even sees women as a cornerstone of patriarchal culture:

Thus in a certain sense the patriarchy creates a particularly rigid matriarchy within the mother-child relationship. Melitta Mitscherlich (1975) points out that a woman can only stop oppressing her children when she becomes aware of her own oppression, and therefore needs no longer pass this on in her actions without reflection. That also means that the woman comes face to face with her suffering. In this way she takes on a central significance in society. She appears as the one who is in the position of being able to break through a vicious circle because she is directly exposed to it and experiences its destructive force in her own body (Melitta Mitscherlich).[1]

4. Women must assert themselves in a culture stamped by male competitiveness, a culture which does not value them in accordance with their achievements (motherhood) and does not accept their ideas of life, while men identify more with this culture and can recognize its norms. Present-day economic problems like the end of unrestricted economic growth and the ecological crisis of the exploitation of nature put the feminist question in a global social context. They present us with the other side of the question, whether patriarchal culture is obsolete and the feminist question is just an alarm signal indicating the need to reorientate our life-style.

Analyses of patriarchy

The term patriarchy, male rule, was only extended to cover this complex conception of oppression during the 1970s. Originally the concept comes from sociology and means 'Rule of the father: a social structure in which the male parent is the head of the family' (*Duden Lexicon*). This meaning is dominant in our academic understanding down to the present day. Alongside it, however, a variant has formed in the psychology of religion, and this has had an influence on the feminist conception of patriarchy. In 1956 Erich Neumann described it in the following way.

From the perspective of this patriarchal aspect which says 'The victory of the man lies in the spiritual principle', the moon and the female element which goes with it is devalued. It is 'only' of the soul, 'only' the supreme form of an earthly and material development as opposed to a 'purely spiritual'

31

one which in its apolitical-Platonic and Jewish-Christian form has led to the severed conceptuality of modern consciousness. However, this modern consciousness threatens the existence of Western humanity, for this one-sidedness of the male development has led to a hypertrophy of the consciousness at the expense of the whole person... The patriarchal consciousness begins from a standpoint in which the spirit is the primarily and *a priori* eternal and pre-given element.[2]

Both conceptions can be found in reflections in the women's movement which began at the end of the 1960s and have now been heightened and intensified by women's experience. From their basic experience that bodily, sexual exploitation of and discrimination against women is the cause of all other oppression, 'patriarchy' has been filled with new content. Three great analyses of patriarchy have been made which draw attention to the sexual, ethical and literary background; the religious and cultural background; and the consequences of male supremacy.

In 1969, in her study *Sexual Politics*, Kate Millett showed that 'our society, like all other historical civilizations, is a patriarchy' and that domination of one sex by the other is deeply rooted in our social structure.

Through this system a most ingenious form of 'interior colonization' has been achieved. It is one which tends moreover to be sturdier than any class stratification, more uniform, certainly more enduring... While patriarchy as an institution is a social constant so deeply entrenched as to run through all other political, social, or economic forms, whether of caste or class, feudality or bureaucracy, just as it pervades all major religions, it also exhibits great variety in history and locale.[3]

The association of sexuality and politics to which she called attention was unusual. According to this, coitus was regarded as a 'prime example of sexual politics on an intimate basis', though the step from the intimate sphere to politics at first seemed enormously large.

In 1973 there followed the religious analysis of patriarchy by the Catholic theologian Mary Daly. After the Second Vatican Council she had hopes for a reform of the church, as she indicated in her book *The Church and the Second Sex*. Now, in *Beyond God the Father*, she dismisses the patriarchy of theology and the church in a radical way.

> The biblical and popular image of God as a great patriarch in heaven, rewarding and punishing according to his mysterious and seemingly arbitrary will, has dominated the imagination of millions for thousands of years. The symbol of the Father God spawned in the human imagination and sustained as plausible by the patriarchy has rendered a service to this type of society by making its mechanisms for the oppression of women appear right and fitting. If God in 'his' heaven is a father ruling 'his' people, then it is in the 'nature' of things and according to divine plan and the order of the universe that society is male dominated.[4]

Theology, she argued, has created an unholy phallic morality which no longer serves life. Daly's hope is directed towards the women who destroy the patriarchal images and dependences in themselves, discover the power of their own being and boldly go against the alleged reality of the patriarchal world and its necrophily: 'Women who reject patriarchy have this power and indeed are this power of transformation that is ultimately threatening to things as they are.'

In 1975 Ernest Borneman provided a comprehensive sexual, ethnological and historical investigation in his classic book *Das Patriarchat*, which he dedicated to the contemporary feminist movement and which was meant to have for them the significance that *Das Kapital* had for the working class. In it he showed how patriarchy came into being and how it was possible to break up all previously dominant systems of social and sexual equality.

The patriarchal clan structure which took shape at a very early stage as a result of the domination of the male who was the one who provided food suggested to the father the idea that he should care for his sons even after his death. The more successful he was as a cattle breeder, and the more he succeeded in getting as many young as possible from each mother animal, the more strongly he felt that his capabilities should be extended to his children. To a much greater degree than agriculture, cattle breeding provokes competition. Where possessions are common property as in the matrilocal, matrilinear clan societies of the old world, no one yet possesses the others. But as soon as the male has discovered private property – and this is now the indisputable 'accomplishment' of the man – he also begins to regard women and children as his 'wife' and his 'children'. Human beings become property. The reification of humanity begins and with it the hostility between the sexes.

For Borneman the tragedy of patriarchy is 'not only man's destruction of himself as a result of the attempt to make woman his slave but the destruction of woman's awareness of herself, the obliteration of all her recollections of her pre-patriarchal past, the blocking of the knowledge of who she once was, is today and can be tomorrow'.[5]

All three analyses of patriarchy are still worth reading because of their personal commitment, their consistency and the wealth of material in them. In a radical way they broke through tabus, and taught people to see the situation of women and the relationship between the sexes in a new light. The detailed investigations made today often no longer take account of them. It is striking – ten years later – what apocalyptic language these earlier investigations all use, the religious modes of expression they employ and the eschatological expectations they cherish. With conceptions like 'cultural

34

revolution' (Millett), 'counter-revolution, male *Putsch*' (Borneman), 'iconoclastic' (Daly), they interpret history and look for change in it. Despite their firm repudiation of Christian culture, religious language creeps in: the present 'wilderness' (Millett), the sisterhood of the 'anti-church' (Daly). Eschatological hopes for a better world without a fixing of sexual roles, an alternative classless culture, a healed women's world, are the secret motive force which will overcome the destructiveness of the patriarchal analyses. Patriarchy is a demonic power which leads to the abyss of existence. In a further analysis *Gyn/ecology*, written in 1981, Daly shows women that they are 'possessed, the possession of the structures of evil and of those who control and legitimate these structures'. Such power can only be countered with opposing forces, for which a religious language is used. Where these powers are not conjured up and mobilized, paralysis and depression will inevitably creep in.

We now know that ending patriarchy will be a laborious, gradual, painful and liberating process. The great utopias that came at the beginning of the women's movement had a function, but with their rigid, radical, martial language and impossible visions in the long run they proved incapable of challenging the everyday world and getting down to details. As early as 1976 Marie-Luise Janssen-Jurreit said of women's utopias: 'If feminism wants to achieve anything as a political power in the next decades it must part company with such eschatological conceptions. No person alive today will experience a realm of freedom – that is the only thing that we know with certainty. By surrending to finalist conceptions of history we refuse to involve ourselves in the extremely threatening imminent future.'[6]

But first of all, how is theology itself related to the religious apocalyptic which is directed against it?

Patriarchy and theology

To judge by the two standard German lexica, the theological preconditions for understanding patriarchy and patriarchalism are very much in need of expansion. The Catholic *Lexikon für Theologie und Kirche* contains only the term 'patriarch', which is used for Israelite ancestors like Noah and Abraham and later for the late Jewish fathers of the faith and the representatives of the hierarchy of the Eastern church. In the Protestant equivalent (*Die Religion in Geschichte und Gegenwart*) there is also a socio-historical 'patriarchalism' which denotes rule within a house and is regarded as 'the most important pre-rational and pre-bureaucratic structural principle'. According to the sociologist Max Weber, patriarchalism is 'one of the most primary types of traditional domination of what is primarily a mostly economic and family association' which ends with the separation of household and work.

It is striking that the two standard works combine a historical survey with this concept, do not refer to the present in any way, and above all do not once mention the conceptions of patriarchal and patriarchalism from the psychology of religion. Even the newest edition of the pocket lexicon *Religion und Theologie* (*TRT*[4]1983) is no exception here. Is this a repression of a still unpleasant confrontation of theology with a structure which it has internalized?

Since the appearance of Johann Jakob Bachofen's *Das Mutterrecht* (1861), which is still worth reading, though it has been challenged, theology cannot really avoid the following fact: father-religions mostly developed late, replaced or even destroyed an earlier 'brotherly' community which was friendly towards the cosmos and democratic, and allied themselves with the social form of patriarchalism which has prevailed to the present day (though Bachofen uses the word 'paternity' here).[7] Bachofen was no isolated phenomenon. He was followed by other investigations[8] which really should have challenged theologians to raise questions relating to the history and psychology of religion. However, theology, built up on belief in Yahweh, which according to the Old Testament condemned all goddesses and nature cults and thus maternal law, was combined so indissolubly in content and structure with a patriarchal model that it could never consider such an 'absurd' question. God was father, the tradition was that of the fathers Abraham, Isaac and Jacob. The church fathers built on this. The pope (papa = father), patriarchs in the Eastern church and Reformation fathers ruled the church, and all who discovered the sisterly charismatic elements in Christianity became the victims of these fathers and had to leave the old mainstream churches.[9]

In 1934 Karl Barth resolutely and undisputedly defended the theological significance of the patriarchy against Henriette Visser't Hooft, who raised critical theological issues in her questions about women. Not only Paul but the whole Bible, he argued, 'in fact does not presuppose matriarchy but patriarchy as the earthly and temporal ordering of the relationship between man and woman'. This was 'a fact, just as it was a fact that the elect people to whom Christ also belonged was not that of the Carthaginians or the Spartans but the people of Israel'.[10] And in an even more basic way, in 1948 he saw the theological significance of patriarchy as being grounded in the historicity of revelation. 'Male action is significant for the world history and characteristic of the world history with which we are acquainted... The biblical witness to revelation assumes this, and subsequent thought in the Christian church has also taken it over without ado.' He makes a distinction between history and nature to the effect that 'the female is as significant for human nature as such as the male is for human history'.[11] In the post-war debate on social ethics, however, theologians explicitly dissociated themselves from a patriarchalism with legalistic roots. Bishop Dibelius wrote to Herr Dehler, the then Minister of the Interior, that the church could not support the 'relative patriarchalism' which could be found in the dominant legislation. However, the 'tendency towards hierarchy' could again be brought up in support of such ordinances. At all events, it was important in Lutheran theology in the last resort to dissociate oneself from social ordinances and to stress equal grace on a neutral, theological level: 'Both in the patriarchal order and in the sphere of equal rights partnership can take shape on the level of equal grace.'[12]

It was more significant, however, that no notice at all was taken of the criticism of patriarchy in terms of the psychology of religion which has been mentioned above, like that of Erich Neumann. His analysis of the domination of the spiritual principle, the victory of the male, had drawn attention only to the devalued female, earthly and material spheres, which were only 'of the soul'. The 'patriarchy of consciousness' which threatened the existence of Western humanity and which is the real concern of theology, the spiritual and pastoral care of the whole man, found no place in theology and therefore not in our *Lexicons* either, under the entry for patriarchy.

With her book *Jesus der Mann*,[13] in 1975 Hanna Wolff made a first breach in theological misunderstanding which was later followed by other investigations by women which took the question further.[14] She showed how here a man – Jesus – had integrated and brought to maturity in himself male and female characteristics and how a patriarchal misunderstanding of Jesus can make God a 'patriarchal monster' and a calculating doctrine of atonement could arise in which God is judge, and guilt and payment are put in the balance. This conception appears 'wherever the masculine turns its back on the feminine and the unconscious because of a lack of concern for integration'. Wolff's book fascinated those who were weary of church doctrine but found it difficult to assert themselves within christology of a traditional kind.

Male perspectives

So far General Secretaries of the World Council of Churches have had a particular concern with theological feminist questions. In 1982 W.A.Visser't Hooft investigated 'The Father-hood of God in an Age of Emancipation'.[15] Here he came to the conclusion that the Fatherhood of God must be maintained because Jesus taught it. For him, however, the Fatherhood of God is 'not a closed or exclusive symbolism. It is open to improvement, enrichment and completion by other symbolic forms like mother, brother, sister, friend.' Here he is anxious about attempts to stop calling God 'he', to depersonalize him, to make him deity or a divine being. For him the difficulty is that he thinks that he himself and the women's movement are still in the time of emancipation, does not comprehend the over-all social criticism of patriarchy in the contemporary women's movement and therefore is above all hostile to a 'lack of social ties'. So his advice that we should come to the Father 'who allows us to live in the glorious freedom of the children of God' seems to women to be an individuated solution which offers them little.

Philip Potter saw the combination of patriarchy and theology more clearly and with more commitment on a visit to England, at Sheffield in 1981.[16] He pointed out that the spiritual ministry which means 'being a servant' has been perverted into hier-archy and patriarchy. One-sided perspectives, interpretations and modes of action have arisen as a result. He pointed out that the reports of the women's study 'The Community of Women and Men in the Church' had made three dualisms more clear to him:

1. The whole division into body and soul – in which the body is often assigned to the woman and men speak with veiled arrogance of the spirit only in male categories – this is a heresy which is even worse than heresy in the life of the church.

2. The division into a private and a public sphere, in which the female is understood to be private and the male public, as a result of which the belief has arisen that the more universal human virtues are private while in the public sphere the law of the survival of the fittest is what counts.

3. The division between humility and power according to

which men have to be concerned with power and women have to be humble. Because people have not been able to connect the two, our humanity has become brutalized and we are exposed to disaster through the arms race and war.

Potter recognized 'the central reciprocal relationship between identity and community'; he understood the contemporary quest by women for their own authentic forms of life and stressed that on the basis of revelation no uniform way and means of life has been laid down by the divine will.

The disastrous, divisive consequences of a patriarchal image, which reduce life to a uniform level and in so doing destroy it, emerge on the fringes of theology where theologians find themselves challenged by women and their own male patterns of thought and conduct thrust aside. All theologians today need to pay intensive attention to the consequences of patriarchal structures which make people ill and destroy them, and take account of the social psychologists, above all of Horst Eberhard Richter.[17] From this perspective men are typical examples of extreme narcissism and the repression of passivity and powerlessness. In the same way as the dominant rational ego deals with external and internal nature, including the passive states of the psyche, so men deal with women and force them to powerlessness and emotionalism. The forces which produce personal and social division run in parallel. Today there is a need to 'recognize and reintegrate those aspects of fragility, weakness and suffering which are suppressed both socially and in the psyche by men in our patriarchal society; or, to put it more precisely, which are repressed psychologically by them with the help of social oppression.' For Richter, the flight of the male before the omnipotent image of God into narcissism and his inability to deal with pain, suffering and powerlessness is a reflection of the God-complex. Asymmetrical, hierarchical primal images of creator/creature, man/woman make it difficult to produce new images of symmetry/equality and non-hierarchical love. Richter's 'God-complex' is a challenge to theology which has yet to be answered.

WHAT IS PATRIARCHY?

Is patriarchy the evil apocalyptic power which threatens to destroy the world? Or have more than just destructive powers been generated in it?

Whatever the answer to the theoretical question, the 'evil' of patriarchy can only be overcome where people discover something of it in themselves and are ready to expose themselves to the painful processes of bringing this to consciousness. For males this means personally being clear about their own patterns of thought and conduct. For theologians this means in addition reflecting their own picture of God in their picture of man. For women this means discovering their share in patriarchy, rising above it, no longer projecting anxiety and powerlessness on to men, churches and societies and making them the scapegoats, and beginning the double task of perceiving and demolishing the divisions and the compulsions to domination in themselves and outside.

Faced with the transportation of the Jewish population from Westerbork to Auschwitz, and with the threat to herself, the young Dutch girl Etty Hillesum wrote: 'Each of us must turn inwards and destroy in himself all that he thinks he ought to destroy in others.'[18]

At first that sounds irreconcilable with women's newly aroused anger about destructive conditions, and irreconcilable with the slogan of the minority movements, 'Destroy what destroys you.' This introversion of this 'violence' may at first terrify others, and it can be seen as a reaction of the time against the brutality experienced all around. It remains important to perceive what is wrong within oneself, to experience oneself as part of the whole, from which alone the whole can be changed. This is a state of maturity from which we do not begin; it is something which must grow and be the aim of all of us. For it is the state of reason, the goddess wisdom, which protects us from irrationality and self-destruction.

Cretan serpent goddess, around 1600 BC *, discovered in the palace at Cnossos*

3

THE FORGOTTEN GODDESS

> Learning to read myth is a distinctive adventure: this art presupposes a gradual change in oneself, a readiness to surrender to a different content of the term 'reality'.
>
> *Christa Wolf*

Women's history

A family which becomes respectable needs a family tree. A nation which becomes aware of itself writes its history. Minorities like the black population in the USA discover their roots in Africa and reflect on their traditions. Anyone who discovers himself or herself needs a past in order to cope with the future. A person cannot be without history. If need be, he or she takes over someone else's history. People need a continuum, something which connects them with their origins and which goes with them into the uncertainty of the future.

Women with both eyes open and learning to stand on both feet are increasingly asking where *their* history is. Of course there are women's histories within traditional history: histories of marriage, love, children, service, tears, being abandoned, pride, hope – almost always related to a partner by whom their life is determined, rarely related to themselves, their programmes and ideas. Women are inessential to the important course of history; they appear as 'his wife' who loved him, was faithful to him, did not understand him or even left him, or gave 'him' children. *Her* ideas, actions, disappointments and decisions are submerged in the great 'we'. Or they are 'the others', those who disrupt marriage, the temptresses, the shadows of the other woman and even less important than the legalized one. According to Virginia Woolf, 'one often catches a glimpse of them in the lives of the great, whisking away into the background, concealing, I sometimes think, a wink, a laugh, perhaps a tear'.[1]

Women's history could be a kind of 'appendix to history', as Virginia Woolf ironically observed, of course without any striking title, so that it is quite appropriate for women to appear in it. But nowadays it is increasingly understood by young women as a counter-history, as a history of the burning of witches and thus as an extermination of the last of the independent, whose daughters had to give evidence against their mothers, and whose self-hatred the crippled self-awareness of women has carried down right to the present day.[2] But alongside history in which we appear 'appropriately' and the history of our self-destruction, women today are rediscovering as their own history the early history of humanity, which is hardly touched on and has been forgotten. It is a history which is seldom related, barely known and never brought to consciousness. It is a history which nowadays affects women deeply, addresses them in their innermost being, restores to them some of their lost identity and opens up perspectives on the future. Anyone who became involved in this process of discovery risked, and indeed still risks, the contempt of his or her caste. For he or she breaks with the academic laws which govern work on written traditions. However, the discovery of early history calls for unconventional methods; it begins, for example, with myths, which can then – as with Heinrich Schliemann – lead to the discovery of Troy. Moreover, it leads further into spheres which our world-view, based on male considerations, often finds disturbing: the 'realm of women' which makes many people anxious and is therefore rejected with derision.

The rediscovery of such women's societies, which are described by ancient writers like Herodotus, Strabo and Diodore, began with the Basle patrician Johann Jakob Bachofen, whom I have already mentioned. 'We are entering... a sphere which awaits its first cultivation', he wrote about his solitary entry into the forms of society which he described as 'maternal law' and which he reconstructed from the reports of ancient writers and the evidence of tomb symbolism.[3] The expression was new and the family conditions which he described were unknown. His book had nothing to do with the emancipation of women but with a great respect for his mother. It was to her that he dedicated it, containing as it did his discovery of fields and broad palaces of inner continents, 'of which those superficial people who exclusively lead an aphis-like two-dimensional existence on the thin upper layer of skin have no inkling'.[4] Right down to the present day a broad range of enlightened bourgeois society has been worried by the terms 'maternal law' or 'matriarchy' without seeing that – according to Bachofen – the child-bearing mother is the source of the 'universal brotherhood of all humanity', that the mother-principle is the foundation of the 'principle of universal freedom and equality', the inviolability of the body, of animals; the principle of peace instead of violence, reconciliation instead of bloody enmity.[5] However, Bachofen's own social stratum, to which he was committed, remained that of patri-archy, and he contrasted the realm of women which he sensitively and passionately described with the law of 'material and corporeal' life, 'paternity' – and with the law of the 'spiritually higher' life. Nevertheless he remains the first witness to an interesting women's history which was first discovered a century later.

The sphere that he had pioneered led in 1932 to the first cultural history of women. The Expressionist writer Berta Eckstein-Diener, who called herself Sir Galahad, was able to build on Bachofen's ethnological researches along with those of Robert Briffault and depict 'a feminine era on the lower seam of history with the priestly, political and economic dominance of the woman':[6] 'A solemn, rich and joyful drama which continues down to our own day and points beyond it.' In the beginning was the woman, and she discovered this principle in the most varied world cultures. Standing close to the Viennese psycho-analytical school, Berta Eckstein-Diener wanted to show women tradition, to practise a 'psychological palaeontology' so that 'she does not appear to have no credentials for what she can do and in fact do'. Only fifty years later, however, did women become aware of their first German-language historian, as they sought their own history.

In the 1950s the emigrant Josephine Schreier wrote her book *Goddesses* in similar solitude and with similar courage in the USA in order to break with traditional history.[7] Although she had no training in ethnology, that became her most important instrument, and she made an independent investigation of the matriarchal culture of the Sumerians. In so doing she came up against the problem how and when male culture took over the properties and functions of the goddesses. This problem of 'identification', which she took over from Freud and applied to the appropriation by men of a female culture, an appropriation which could be described in either negative or positive terms, became a key question for her. Over against the Expressionist account of history in Berta Eckstein-Diener, by means of her 'psychological palaeontology' she penetrated into the process of male identification with the goddess, myths and their control, in a great variety of forms of patriarchal culture from philosophy to mathematics.

The findings demonstrated by both women, namely the integrity of feminine primal history which for the two of them was part of the history of the self, an example of coming to terms with existing in patriarchal isolation, has meanwhile been abundantly advanced by later research:

1. Investigations in the Near East in Jericho and Anatolia have disclosed an early Stone-Age cultural stratum which indicates that the mother-goddess attested by later mythologies must have been preceded by feminine cults with female stone figures, the work of female artists. For example, in Catal Hüyük there are small ancestor-images in the strata from the sixth to the eighth millennia BC made out of clay, female breasts

put side by side in series, bas-reliefs of women in the posture of giving birth, and also wall paintings. Similar finds show that even before the beginning of mother religion proper, matriarchal religion covered the whole Mediterranean basin and its hinterland.[8]

2. Investigations in French caves have put in question the old theory that the drawings of bulls, oxen and bisons are hunting symbols from a male culture. Marie König interprets them as symbols of the moon, i.e. as a reflection of the waxing and waning phases of the moon.[9] Thus portrayals of bulls with vulva signs are evidence of a matriarchal religion. Representations of bulls in caves or bulls' horns stand for the moon and thus for the great mother goddess, and ultimately for rebirth.

3. In palaeo-linguistics (research into human language in primal history), which understands language as a record of the early history of humanity, attention is drawn to a preponderance of feminine terms. In the archaic word roots *gal-*, *kal-* and so on, which even now shape all languages, which denote cave, dwelling, covering, mother's body, clan, birth, and therefore have feminine origins, there is nothing comparable for the man. This indicates a far-distant social dominance of the woman which lasted for a long time.[10]

4. Research into folk-tale and myth as carried out by Heide Göttner-Abendroth shows that folk tales, like myths, are reflections of the complex practice of archaic societies, and thus could also be reflections of matriarchal societies. The matriarchal world-view lasted into patriarchal societies and their great religions, above all in lower social strata and marginal groups. Accordingly a 'latent matriarchal opposition' can be found right down to the Middle Ages.[11]

Much research has been done by males who have no special interest in women and their quest for identity. But many interpretations are to be attributed to women themselves, their insight and their experience of themselves. The cave paintings which Marie König interpreted have been seen in a new light in the context of their elemental capacity to show the early understanding of the connection between death and life. Language which males wanted to interpret as male hunting cries proves from the perspective of feminine scholarship to be a means of communication between mother and child.

Over against the classical theory which has so far shaped Western education, intellectual attitudes and the cult of personality, we now have a revolutionary new definition of our culture. This means a completely new orientation for people who previously were stamped by the 'higher principle' of paternity.

Traces of women's cultures

All the cultures known to us at present seem to have been preceded by matristic, mother-centred cultures. This can be demonstrated from the Tibetan women's kingdom *via* the two Americas to the Scandinavian peoples. The quite different traces of these cultures can be followed right down to the present, even if they so far have achieved a significance which is in complete contrast to their original meaning. One example is our folk tales, where the dominant powers who determine fate are fairies and wise women, although for a long time wise men have dominated our economics and politics. And another can be found in Greece, where travellers see how beneath the upper layer of sanctuaries of Zeus and Apollo the snake revered in matriarchal cultures had its home and the priestess Pythia spoke the oracle.

The period at which these old cultures were replaced by a society dominated by male symbols and values varies. For example, in Mexican civilization a male culture very soon won over and integrated an early matristic stratum. In ancient Europe this presumably happened between 2000 and 3000 BC as a result of Indo-Germanic shepherd and warrior tribes who invaded the Mediterranean basin from the north.

However, thanks to its position as an island, Crete long maintained its old culture and created a society which was greatly influenced by women; this can be reconstructed and still proves fascinating. Egypt, too, was largely spared this revolution. The structures remained matristic, and were either dominated by women or egalitarian. Presumably women inherited power and bestowed it on men.

Among the Celts and Ires we still find in the Middle Ages remnants of female succession and concepts of goddesses which proved hard to suppress. The transitions from matristic to patriarchal cultures often took place over centuries or even millennia. Mixed forms were long the rule. Mother cults would continue to be practised for a long time in societies shaped by men, or below an upper level of religion dominated by males a religious subculture like the Shaman cult practised especially by 'ordinary people' could continue, e.g. in Japanese Shintoism. Usually, however, religion and social structures corresponded, or at least developed the tendency to adapt to each other; here economic forces determined the trend. At all events we can note that from 2000 in the European sphere patriarchalizing processes can be observed which were played out on various levels and had come into full flood by the end of the Middle Ages. These were processes in which cultures orientated on the woman and thus primarily on the goddess were replaced by those which were related to the male and thus primarily to male gods. In these transitions the cyclical dying-and-rising symbol of the moon was replaced by the symbol of the sun, expressing the spirit and victory of the understanding.

The left side, the one preferred in all cultures which reckon by nights, was replaced by the right, the male, the calculating side. Left became left-wing, politically suspect. Right was right. The serpent, which sheds its skin, representing rebirth, the power of healing, new life and in its circular form completion (see plate on p.42), became the dangerous monster symbolizing drives, uncontrollable nature, temptation, which has to be killed (see 109f.). Hera, who previously was an independent goddess dominating pre-Hellenic Greece, now sprang as the warlike Pallas Athene from the head of Zeus. Women moved back from the centre to the periphery of the cult; for a long time they were able to remain as priestesses and prophetesses, but then they finally lost their cultic function, above all with Christianity, which developed in a patriarchal and hierarchical way. There was a parallel development with nature: in symbols of the moon and the snake which still stamped existence, it was first bound and then subjected, in the victory of the sun and the fight with the dragon. However, these processes, which can be noted in almost all cultures, take very different courses, sometimes integrating, often domesticating and sometimes preserving bipolarity. Only the one-sided development of solar-masculine Christianity had the sharpest and most marked effect here and destroyed the balance which had often been preserved between the traditional matristic elements and the patriarchal elements which displaced them.

Women's societies

As compared with 'late' patriarchy, which is only 3000 years old, matristic or matriarchal cultures have a history of at least 4000 years to show. In the view of many scholars, men and women, they preceded our Western culture. They extended from the Danube, the Black Sea and the Caucasus south to the Mediterranean and the Persian Gulf, areas which are special spheres for matriarchal scholarship old and new, and they embrace different stages of development from the Stone Age to the Bronze Age.

In broad outline the following picture emerges. Both in the gathering period, when as a feeder and gatherer she had an important function for the clan, and at the beginning of the agricultural period, where in a later phase she presumably invented the hoe and hoeing, woman had a dominant or at least an egalitarian position. Both phases, the gathering period and the early agriculture period, merge meaningfully into each other. In both there is a need for the woman's attention to the earth, to plants, fruits and seeds. The production of food from vegetables and the observation that new growth emerges from cores which are left over and thrown away go hand in hand. The digging implement of the early gatherers with which they dug up tubers, mushrooms, plants and also worms, and with which the first holes were made for planting seeds, has been called the 'woman's sceptre' (Gordon Childe). As the one who gives birth and feeds she is the primal producer and the 'mother of civilization' (Ernest Borneman). In the hunting period but also at the beginning of sedentarization her position was undisputed.

What she developed and possessed belonged to the tribe. Private property was still unknown and can only be demonstrated from a later period when decorations, hoes and cooking utensils were put in graves with the dead. The male fished and hunted, and was incorporated into the tribe in which the mother and her successors guaranteed continuity in the community.

With the invention of the plough, and the increased production and the law of property which followed, and also as a result of the profitability of cattle breeding, interest grew in male succession and these early matrilinear (maternal succession) and matrilocal (maternal dwelling) communities with their unwritten laws vanished. With the plough the male became the dominant procurer of food and also had greater autonomy over against the clan, which was still necessarily interdependent in the period of elementary agriculture. The smaller clan unit developed with the farmstead. This made it possible to take note of family connections: whereas in the clan unit the child's father was not decisive, now he was known.

With the economic domination of the male, his sexual domination also began. He discovered that he was the giver of seed; he became aware of his property and his productive power. The prohibition against incest arose. His children now entered into a succession, became part of himself, his property, and in this structure his wife lost her functions as primal mother, feeder and landowner. She became dependent on his claim to productive power. In a developed agricultural phase she became 'an appendix of his presence' (George Thompson).

That, in the broadest of terms, is the development of patriarchy, though developments varied greatly over long periods of time and in individual areas.[12] We must bear in mind the connection between economy and sexuality: the loss of an order in which the sphere of the woman was great and the development of a new family order which was accompanied by sexual laws and a reduction in the woman's function.

The roots of patriarchal developments already lie in agricultural culture. But the invasion of the Indo-Europeans, with their cattle economy above all run by men, and an order predominantly built on male functions, then brought about the final loss of the old matriarchal culture.

In the meantime, criticism has been voiced against clearly-stated theories about the course of history, matriarchal myths and the dreams of women which arise out of them. Uwe Wesel, for example, infers from historical investigation that there were indeed egalitarian societies, societies without patriarchy and with matrilinearity and matrilocality in Crete, Egypt and Lycia: 'At the periphery of Graeco-Roman antiquity there are societies which at all events were not patriarchal.'[13] Women were in a better position there than in Greece, Rome or elsewhere in the West. But there was no matriarchate here – the rule of women in the original literal sense. Similarly, because of individual investigations leading to different results he doubts whether a general female culture preceded patriarchal culture everywhere. In his view, at all periods women were at a disadvantage as a result of pregnancy, neotenia (entry into sexual maturity) and the division of work arising out of that. He therefore sees the only solution of the feminine question in the removal of any division of work, not only in employment and pay, 'but also in the economic unit of the family, in housekeeping and in looking after children', rather

52

than in a retrospective concern for matriarchy. However, he too accepts that there were matrifocal societies where women stood at the centre of social and religious life, where they organized their work themselves, where the children were assigned to their kin and the settlement was organized according to female customs. Women were usually admitted to cults but also had their own cults. One example of a matrifocal culture which has been investigated is that of the Hopi Indians, among whom women have a strong position, and significantly acts of violence cannot be demonstrated either between men or by men against women.[14] The word 'matriarchal' should therefore be more aptly replaced by 'matrifocal' or 'gynocentric', in order not to give too simple an idea of the régime. Nevertheless, for the rest of this book I prefer to use the linguistically simpler word 'matriarchal' for female cultures and women's traditions.

For some women, too, the 'myth of matriarchy' is meanwhile 'nothing but a tool to keep women in their place'.[15] 'What use is it for women,' Marie-Luise Janssen-Jurreit asked, 'if they console themselves over the oppression which has now lasted for millennia with the notion that at the beginning of human history they dominated men?'[16]

The goddess today

For many women, however, images and conceptions of the goddess have had a helping or even healing religious function in their experiences of powerlessness. 'She exists, not to cajole or to reassure the male, but to assert herself' (Adrienne Rich).[17] She reflects the basic human experiences of birth and death, life and passing on. She is the mother who gives life, but at the same time she is also the earth mother to whose womb men and women go home in death. Different symbols which express this basic experience accompany her: the moon in its threefold form, waxing, full and waning; the bull between whose horns the full moon is set; the moon-shaped double axe

– which is not an instrument of murder; the pot, the vessel which corresponds to the body, from which new life comes, the pot in which she gathers and stores food, which becomes a tomb to which a man or woman returns – hidden, as in the mother's womb. It is the world in which people live, limited, surveyable; for 'the mother's realm is always of this world'. Death and life are transcended in her, not yet separated through experiences of guilt, punishment and alienation.

In contrast to the male heaven, from which a God reigns, the goddess represents for women a kind of principle within the world. She is the world, revealed in every woman:

> The image of the Goddess inspires women to see ourselves as divine, our bodies as sacred, the changing phases of our lives as holy, our aggression as healthy, our anger as purifying... Through the goddess, we can discover our strength, enlighten our minds, own our bodies, and celebrate our emotions. We can move beyond narrow constricting roles and become whole.[18]

Whereas our traditional images of goddesses with their patriarchal stamp emanate classical beauty and youth, the early goddess embraces all three phases of human life. The attractive Venus or the suckling Isis have been encouraged and perpetuated in various ways in patriarchal religions, and the portrayal of the Christian Mary as a beautiful young mother has profited much from this. But the old woman, wise and near to death, full of experience, rich in knowledge of nature and its power, who combines wisdom and knowledge, comes to appear only in matriarchal strata of art, myth and folk-tale: as the wise woman of a story, in the person of Athene with the owl, the symbol of light and knowledge, and as the snake goddess, image of healing power and return. In patriarchal religions men take over this sphere: knowledge becomes science, the wisdom of old age is depicted as a wise old man, and the wise women are finally suspected of magic, burnt as witches and eliminated.

The goddess resting in herself, who is no reflection of a world shaped by men, also forms her own relationships. It is in accordance with the social structure of matriarchal culture that it is not the husband of the family but the brother of the woman within the clan and above all the daughter of the woman who underlies the tradition and who plays the major roles. The old epic of Demeter and Persephone, in which the daughter is abducted from the mother into the underworld and the mother responds by refusing fertility until the daughter is returned, contains something of these relationships. In Eleusis these mysteries were still celebrated at a late stage as a relic of a past relationship.

In our culture, by contrast, the problems associated with father and son are the depth-psychological model to which even the problems associated with women are subordinated. Abraham and Isaac, but not Sarah and Isaac, Sarah and Hagar, are the models to which we relate. The manifold relationships of women in friendship, affinity and shared work are hardly reflected. Psychology today shows that precisely this repression of the positive mother-daughter relationship focussed on independence and worth is determinative of the ominous transmission of male desires for pliant women.

The man is regarded in different ways in his relation to the goddess. He can be seen as a phallic symbol, as a hero who dies and rises again with nature in her womb. The male principle is thus embedded in the female universe (Göttner-Abendroth). However, as Judith Ochshorn argues, in polytheistic religion he can also represent fertility independently of the goddess. Dualistic understandings of sexuality emerged first with monotheism. Up to that point god and goddess did not represent the 'male' or the 'female' respectively, but both together expressed the wealth of the divine being, the one as a man and the other as a woman. This at least prevented the exclusion of the woman from the cult.[19]

The results of research into matriarchy

Regardless of whether the goddess and a retrospective survey of female society help women to find their identity in history, or even have a religious healing function which brings with it forms of worship like those to be found above all in the Goddess movement in the USA, at all events research into matriarchy seems to me to contribute important features to the discovery and orientation of women.

1. It teaches us another perspective which, beyond our rational analytical capacities, discloses new sources of human, female history which can be read in symbols, images and myths.

2. It shows us the picture, which has been almost forgotten in our culture, of the independent woman with an intrinsic value who – also as a goddess – represents totality, life and creative force in numerous statuettes, statues, myths and images: a reflection of women's history, women's relationships, everyday experiences in cult, society and family.

3. It draws our attention to patriarchalizing processes in which the independent image of the women is taken over or even demonized. Heide Göttner-Abendroth has demonstrated this patriarchal loss of the original totality of the woman by means of the three well-known goddesses Artemis, Aphrodite and Athene. All initially represented those three phases of life which at the same time denoted heaven, earth and underworld. Then an aspect of this totality was isolated and finally devalued:

> Thus Artemis became the chaste huntress daughter of Zeus, Aphrodite the exalted *hetaira* and Athene the divine housewife, ceding her wisdom of age to Zeus. This change in the image of goddesses ran parallel to the changes in the social position of the woman in Hellenistic Greece. Like the goddesses their places were indicated by the male definitions of virgin, prostitute and housewife.[20]

This process is to be observed at other points than in the transition from matristic to patriarchal society. It also lurks in every movement with egalitarian beginnings. It can also be noted in the three most important female figures of the New Testament, Mary, Mary Magdalene and Martha. And down to the present it can be observed in many revivalist movements. A converse process never took place.

4. It can make us aware of our psychological matriarchy and make us sensitive to the processes in ourselves. A 'terror of rediscovery' (Christa Wolf) has seized many women in that they discover behind inculcated modes of behaviour which have now become questionable a psychological world of their wishes and dreams which has always existed. Anyone who enters it self-critically, lovingly and with patience can experience this archetypal world of totality and wholeness. Memories arise as to when and where it became sullied, when we dismissed it as naive, irrational, unscientific and childish, when the last rebellions between the inculcated self and the authentic self took place.

When women practise this psychological palaeontology they come up against their capacity for integration, for bringing together forms of art, making connections, engaging in something of cosmic dynamics. But in the course of our rational education we have learned to give priority to analytical capacities and to neglect other forces. For Adrienne Rich it is important no longer simply to enquire of the learned, trained intellect but to ask, 'What do my own brain, my own body tell me – my memories, my sexuality, my dreams, my power, my energy?'[21] Where we rediscover the basis of our overall capacity to see things together and make connections we can develop and mature.

Another sphere is our feeling of community which was once significant for holding together the clan, but which we must fill with new content. To experience and receive oneself from others, to develop autonomy in community, is not a loss of autonomy but an extension of our personality.

A third sphere is our pragmatic down-to-earthness. It is part of our nature as earth mothers. It is a matter of turning to the small and the smallest, as the symbol for the great. It can become pettiness, but if instead of putting forward principles we allow ourselves to be moved by things and people themselves, we practise this nearness to the earth which makes us grasp our problems in a more realistic way.

Over a long period of having been given a subordinate place in society women have developed a system which for long secured them respect and a degree of 'wholeness'. In a system of subculture they 'developed a progressive inward and therefore authentic system of values' (Jean Baker Miller)[22], with their capacities for integration, the formation of communities and pragmatism. However, they did so without reward and only with occasional recognition. In this way they penetrated to the depths of humanity and in so doing preserved something in their patriarchal alienation. Today, when we are well aware of the destruction of ourselves and nature, the contempt for the body and for women in the patriarchy, when sub-cultures are rising to the surface, the connections betwen women's values, the preservation of nature and the change that we need in our society are becoming clear. It is not a matter of re-establishing the matriarchy, nor of a sad glimpse backwards. What is important is to secure those modes of access to life which have been kept from us. The domination of women which has become archetypally visible, the domination of women with their wealth of capabilities, imprisoned in the cage of their homes, exercises pressure on society to introduce in a new form that for which it is made. Today we are at the beginning of a new period of society where an ideology and world-view which exploit nature must give way to a society in which domination is demolished and interdependence can be seen. We can become aware who we are and can devote ourselves to the painful yet beautiful process of self-discovery. Women have an advantage here in their capacity for perception. And they have the chance to counter the devouring aspect of the great mother which men so fear with that which mothers, having been made powerless, could not achieve: with detachment despite proximity, with the capacity for conflict despite harmony, with solitude despite community.

Matriarchy without social domination, the goddess or religious claims can help us to discover ourselves anew. To discover myth as a document of a hitherto invisible history and to learn to read it is – according to Christa Wolf – 'an adventure', and it presupposes the readiness 'to devote oneself to another content of the term "reality"'.[23]

Part Two: Critical Theology

*The crucified liberation. Painting by Gloria Guevara
(Solentiname)*

4

FEMINIST THEOLOGY

It is an adventure (to be a woman) which calls for so much courage; a challenge which never becomes too much. You will have to undertake so much if you come into the world as a woman. Thus for a start, you will have a fight over asserting that God, if there is one, could just as well be an old white-haired woman or a beautiful girl. You will have a fight over saying that sin did not come into being on the day when Eve picked the apple; that on that day a wonderful virtue was born which is called disobedience. Finally, you will have a fight to demonstrate that in your smooth and healthy body there is an intelligence which cries out to be heard... It will be very hard for you to cry this out, and you will often, almost always, draw the short straw. But you must not lose heart.

Oriana Fallaci

The model of liberation theology

In the 1960s, minorities throughout the world – blacks, Latin American farm-workers, Indians – became aware of how little their social and personal situation was affected by the traditional theology and praxis of the church. At the beginning of the 1970s the first models of liberation theology emerged in which the disadvantaged groups sought to understand their oppression and their expectations of liberation afresh in the light of the gospel. Once they had begun to fight for their indepedence they recognized that the God who was proclaimed to them by white men was not an expression of their feelings, their longing for liberation and redemption. The Jesus who was to be their brother had the face of their colonial master.

Where was their God? Was the God of the white oppressor not the God who was the cause of their dependence, who guaranteed their oppression? Where was the God who stood by their side in the battle against unjust conditions, who freed them, who broke open their prison, as Jesus had said in the messianic promise in Luke 4.18 (see plate, p.62).

In parallel to this, women, who from the end of the 1960s had been engaged in the feminist movement against sexism, the oppression of one sex by the other, began to develop a feminist theology.[1] Where and how could theology support and accompany them in their fight against male rule? Where was theology itself so male dominated that it was no use for freeing women? How could a religious and political spirituality develop which helped women in the search for their identity?

American women who saw how minority theologies developed in their own country and who unlike their European sisters were more practised and socially versed in theology, led the way and still are providing the decisive stimuli towards thought. In the middle of the 1970s the light spread over to Europe and meanwhile it has produced a growing grass-roots movement of feminist theology which flourishes above all in places of work and autonomous groups.

However, in German society there has long been mistrust of the term 'feminism'. In contrast to the USA, for us the word feminism is fraught with a fear of aggression, anarchy, misandrism. Hitherto it was almost completely unknown, and in our first women's movement it played only a marginal role, whereas for example in Anglo-Saxon countries, thanks to their older democratic tradition, minority programmes like feminism were more easily accepted. All attempts to replace this word, which is so fraught with aggression and which seems so 'frivolous' alongside the 'serious' word theology, have so far failed. 'Theology of women for women' or 'feminine theology' does not convey anything about the social situation without which feminist theology is unthinkable.

At the first European consultation of Christian women

64

in Europe (Brussels 1978), women aware of this conflict attempted a definition of their own.

> Feminism for us is a strategy, a principle of life, by which our thought and action are determined. Women in Western countries are primarily concerned to discover themselves as women. Since society and church have for centuries laid down who they are and what they have to do and not do, it is now time that they themselves should discover who they are, what they can do and what they want to do.
>
> This process is bound up with a critical consideration of the structures of their churches and the societies in which they live...
>
> It is our common concern mutually to have the courage to show ourselves, our ideas, our plans, our wishes, indeed our emotions, in our churches and our societies and to articulate them with the aim of a change which can be described in the following terms: church and theology should be more total, put in a position to take account of all people, and especially the oppressed.
>
> We emphatically stress that this strategy, this principle of living, is not directed against the male but is rather meant to encourage him to discover his pole in the opposite sex. We wish to live in friendship with him and to gain him as a covenant partner on the way to liberation.[2]

Here feminism had abandoned its claim to absoluteness, had moved from being a principle to being a way of life, from being a world-view to being a strategy. Since then 'feminist theology' has become an established conception internationally and in the ecumenical world, one which can no longer be rejected and with which we must come to terms.

Behind the mistrust in our country, however, there is more than taking offence at terminology. In our tradition, theology, talk of God, was above all talk of the transcendent 'wholly other', sovereign God. To see him as the object of critical debate in an unattractive group of women is regarded in some

Christian circles as being close to blasphemy. We are only slowly becoming aware in our culture which for so long has been closed, of the rights that minorities have to their own forms of expression, and it is taking us even longer to allow the hundred blossoms of different images of God slowly to bloom in our strictly ordered theology. The handicapped, youth, students, the old, children – how do they experience God and what do they have to contribute to theology? Where is their theology? These questions are seldom asked in universities, but they are very much alive at church conferences and organizations, above all where the ghetto is opening up. Before we turn to feminist theology we must touch briefly on the basic notions of a primal model of minority theology, black theology.[3]

When in the 1960s the coloured population in the USA began to fight for their rights, one element in this fight was often that of their own religious traditions which had helped them to survive over centuries of slavery. Here their own 'black' history and religious spirituality were brought to consciousness. From the underground of their history notions grew up of their power, their capacities for resistance. The image of Uncle Tom, the devout servant of his master and God, was replaced with that of the black militant, who took a stand for his worth and for the just cause of the population which had been deprived of their human rights. The black Christ replaced the image of the white Son of God. This theology found a place in the hearts, hands and heads of those who had previously been dependent, and changed them. Three principles which distinguish black from traditional theology and which we shall also meet again in feminist theology, emerge here:

1. The starting point of theological thought and action is the experience of social oppression.

2. The goal of theology is human worth, the possibility of being a person within a just order of society.

66

3. Theology is praxis. Theology takes place in just action and the struggle for a new society.

This put in question a Western Protestant theology which begins from the sinful individual, which is concentrated more on the separation of the two kingdoms of spiritual and secular experience than on society, which reflects the inner certainty of salvation more than political justice, and for which struggle as Christian praxis is an alien category.

Many people found the consequences of the Latin American theology of liberation much more serious and disquieting. For liberation theologians, the question how an 'unperson' who cannot read and write and who does forced labour can understand himself or herself as a child of God, can only be resolved in a liberated society. Many of them find an analysis of contemporary society in the Marxist theory of society. We also find Marxist theories in feminism and in feminist theology. But they are not fundamental to the Christian praxis of liberation. There are various concepts for changing society. In feminist theology they can extend from liberalism via a Socialist feminism to radical feminism.[4]

Theologies of liberation open up a new context for theology. However conditioned by time and social context these theologies may appear at first sight, they take up the Jesus experience of being cast out, of being abandoned by God, of death. They show how existential and concrete a matter it is to be a new person, how there is no reflection without action, no inner peace without fighting for peace. The theologies of liberation moved from the old ancestral home into a new promising land. They are promising because they can offer models of livable life and healing action instead of scepticism about society and inner withdrawal, in changing societies where individuals are isolated and new groups are forming.

The experience of women

Thus feminist theology is not dogmatics. It cannot be arranged in theological *loci* and develops a dynamic of its own. It is first of all a movement which despite a common goal is also shaped by a variety of groups with a variety of experiences. These groups shape the questions and developments of feminist theology. To begin with they were led by women who as a result of the feminist challenge were chiefly concerned with the problems of repressed sexuality and the violence of men in the church which was never talked about. These were joined by many people who could not identify with the churches' orientation on partners and marriage because they were house-wives, lived alone or were single parents. There were also a large number of Catholic women who could not expect any equal status in the hierarchical structure of their church and who felt hemmed in by its particularly restrictive sexual morality. The angry, the homeless and those without rights were then joined in a second phase by women from the churches who felt a deeply disturbing tension between being a woman and being a Christian, a tension which threatened to tear them apart. They rejected radical solutions, and still felt very strongly associated with the Christian tradition, but looked for new forms of life and new possibilities of expression. The curious and the hungry, to whom the churches are intrinsically completely alien, but who look for their own religious forms of expression, whether pantheistic, humanistic or anthroposophical, were also a constant element in the picture.

However, like liberation theology, which has opened up a new area where theology is being done, feminist theology has also developed new methods both in the academic world[5] and in theological praxis. It has become an instrument which gives us credentials for asking about the repressed reality of women and the reality of God in society, church and theology. The three principles which distinguish liberation theologies from traditional theology also hold for feminist theology. To make them more easily comprehensible, I would now also like to apply them to feminist theology.

1. The starting point of theological thought and action is the experience of oppression in society.

If the word 'oppression' sounds too portentous, it could be replaced by narrowing or neglect. But the situation remains the same, whatever word we use: women in our bourgeois prosperous society lack social, economic and legal recognition, and this has psychological consequences. Women's suffering – however varied it may seem – was for a long time internalized; it kept women humble and perhaps made them sensitive to others, thus producing for many people the ideal of the lovable, passive, patient woman. But once we are clear how suffering cripples people and how much suffering arises out of social injustice which can be done away with, we must regard the pressure of suffering on women as oppression, a negative factor, and work for it to be removed. Political theologies have made Christians aware of social conditions. Christians can no longer leave these to the 'authorities' and the patience of the oppressed. Church, theology and individual Christians can no longer avoid the fact that they have responsibility for social structures. All injustice goes against the justice of God and his coming kingdom. We cannot pray 'Thy kingdom come' and retreat into our own inner spheres. Because we are accepted and just before God, we are also responsible for all unjust structures in our society.

The question is, what status does such experience of women have for theological discourse? 'Experience' first of all appears to have a subjective, biographical stamp. It has no 'objective status' and can be suspected of being irrelevant and in this case also 'unreliably feminine'!

Experience is partial, but in our case it takes on another status as the experience of a group. If we take seriously the different experiences of groups which are coming of age, then the varied experiences of women, who in fact are still in the majority in our populations, have an important function. The experience is not always called 'discrimination', but the 'shortfall' suffered by women, in whatever form, can always be seen under the surface of every woman, however independent she may feel. And if it is not – at this point there should be the beginning of some solidarity with other sensitive women whose sufferings are severe. For Christians are those who have become sensitive – we used to say compassionate. The experiences of others could extend and clarify something of women's history where there have been other forms of oppression or violation.

The difficult question is whether we can speak of God from our experiences. God, the wholly other, God the one who is revealed in Christ – what has he to do with this suffering? He speaks from the Bible, he speaks by his Son, he speaks through the pastor in the pulpit – how can he speak through women? Are not all encounters with God bound up with a conversion experience? With a lightning flash from above? A voice from beyond? A break with all my 'needs' as a self?

There will always be different experiences of God. The socially conditioned experiences of women today are authentic, real and oppressive. They shed light on a group of children of God who have fallen short in what is due them in a Christian West and in a Christian church. They are part of a history of suffering in which there is still something of God's suffering in and to the world.

In my view this is the context of the idea of a revelation of God in women which often emerges in feminist theology; it is also its limitation. Experience of injustice is reflected in the story of Jesus and can represent the story of Jesus. However, not every complaint from women has the character of revelation. The story of Jesus which tells of exemplary mutuality, surrender and selfhood is the criterion by which we become sensitive and perceptive to human experiences and parallels.

Being a person

2. The centre of theological reflection is human worth, being a person in a just order of society. If in our present traditional church theology we speak of people as the starting point for theological reflection, we are speaking of the introverted – sinful – seeker after God, the person who rebels against God or the person in his or her duality, as a partner, who is directed towards the other and only in that way fulfils his or her humanity. Feminist theology is interested in another process: the process of liberation, the developing wholeness of the woman in a social, patriarchal alienation and the overcoming of that alienation. So the basic presupposition of feminist theology is not the existence of the individual as a sinner. Pragmatically its concern is to counter contemporary pressures which get in the way of true humanity. So in this process of liberation the accent is on the complete recovery of the status of being a child of God, a status which is lost in oppressive structures.

If we accept this approach, theological perspectives emerge to which we always fail to do justice:

We *are* children of God, daughters of God.

We *are* partners of God, as women, called to work with him in this world.

We *are* God's good creation.

This shift in our perspective follows from the consequences of theological developments: preaching about our limitations, and above all about the limitations of women. Virtually every theological discussion among women in the German context raises this question in a basic way. For women, preaching has become preaching about out limitations: limitations which are set by husband, children, the social order. The gospel is experienced as a tie and thus as limitation, hardly as liberation and expansion.

When there is talk today of the 'self-realization' of women, it comes up against the general social, Christian, patriarchal anxiety that boundaries are being violated and a social order is being destroyed. It would make sense once again to investigate the psychological significance and general devaluation of this conception. Individuation – which is what self-realization means – is accepted in the psychological and theological sphere. But is it not applicable to women? Men have attempted to realize it in a patriarchal society – often at the expense of women. But when women seek their identity and a life of their own, a life which is not determined by others but is meaningful for them, they are told that the same behaviour is egoism. This may happen through anxiety over losing power and privileges, and perhaps also traditional attention and concern. However, there is no justification for the charge – on quite different grounds.

If one talks to women who still dare to use this controversial word of themselves it becomes evident that they are thinking in terms of scope for self-development rather than seeking elbow room in which they can impose themselves by force. Women experience their selfhood in a network of relationships. In both love and work their selfhood is experienced within this web of relationships. In the last century the American Elizabeth Cady Stanton could say of this self-understanding: 'Self-realization is a higher duty than self-sacrifice'. Here there is a clash between different experiences, different male and female conceptions. However, it seems to me symptomatic that nowadays many women are already withdrawing themselves, are against 'self-realization' and bowing to a male culture and terminology. This is the result of an idea of order which quite evidently makes its mark on women in our culture.

Women's contempt for the body and thus contempt for themselves, which can be explained from a patriarchal understanding of themselves and the world, is another reason which has led us to look at our daughterhood and partnership with God. As long as we have not completely freed ourselves from the Eve tradition, as long as we see the human body as a centre of negative drives, we continue to despise ourselves and will have to set out boundary posts. Until theology has integrated the insights of the psychology of integrated people, in whom soul and body live in friendship, no matter what statements it may make, it has failed to understand the question of women. This theory of 'fallen creation' and the 'black pedagogy'[6] practised above all against children and women in the church tradition is not just past history. It is a reality which extends right down to our own day.

It seems almost a threat to our traditional patterns of I-Thou, partner, husband-wife for the woman to appear as an individual in feminist theology. However, for many women it is liberating no longer to be over against, no longer to be the object – usually – of male thought, and instead to be the subject, actually the subject of theology.

Action and reflection

3. Theology is praxis. Action and reflection affect each other reciprocally. Theology takes place in just action and in the struggle for a new society. If we have been brought up in the traditional scheme we distinguish between theology and praxis: theology is thought, praxis is action. Anglo-Saxon and Third-World theologies were already orientated on praxis. In pietism we had the *praxis pietatis*, which seemed more important than the abstract speculation cherished and tended by theologians. Women in our history have also preferred commitment to reflective theologizing. So far what has been specifically done in the church for women is often more important than any theological thinking. Church structures often seem to be impenetrable, repressive and highly super-fluous. Women – having attained positions of responsibility in the church – have often survived with a minimal theology, but in so doing have also surrendered something of themselves. If we do not remember that, our action becomes no more than menial work. If we separate the spheres of action and reflection we sin against totality, violate our rational capacities and resign

73

ourselves to being women who surrender themselves and fall apart as real persons.

Feminist theology, which is practical theology, is fascinating for women because *women* are reflecting their situation, are acting as women who are aware of themselves, are becoming clear about themselves and experiencing their own liberation in liberating action towards others. The action is constantly bound up with reflection; just as something of life is suppressed in women, so too it is suppressed in others, and should revive again. Work in women's hostels, with the underprivileged, self-experience groups with women, banana actions for the Third World, boycotting of fruit from South Africa are endorsed, justified and given theological significance.

At the same time this implies more perception of responsibility for the world. Just as I am made the good, whole creation of God, so society has a goal and a promise: the liberation of the oppressed. Anyone who is at the margin, in a position without responsibility, now becomes someone who acts with responsibility; the oppressed is not a passive object of the compassion of others but an agent who can encounter depression and resignation and who has a vision which gives a future to her and to others.

This makes obsolete the old formula which derives from Reformation theology about the relationship between justification and sanctification, a formula which has been discussed *ad nauseam*. In ourselves, in the totality of our experience, knowledge and action can become one and we can be clear about what is 'right' and where it is leading. Since we 'understand with the body' (Christa Wolf), we set new standards for thought and action.

If liberation theologies have helped us to see divided human experience as one more consequence of wrong social developments and to see the personal worth of humanity as being on the side of God, a new element arises with feminist theology:

1. There is a reawakening of sensitivity to the forgotten dimensions, to the spheres of the senses, the psyche, the body,

the imagination, which hardly had any status in an abstract intellectual theology. Feminist theology continues the humanizing of theology in an unprecedented way.

2. The substance of theology, which has hardly been criticized by liberation theologies, can now be investigated clearly in respect of its masculine imagery, its masculine vehicles (the Bible) and its hierarchical structures (the church). Feminist theology thus inaugurates a real renewal of theology.

*The last communion of St Mary Magdalene in penitential dress.
Tiefenbronn altar by Lucas Moser, 1431*

5

THE BIBLE AND FEMININE SELF-AWARENESS

> He (the man) has appropriated for himself the privilege of
> Jehovah by claiming the right to determine her sphere of life,
> whereas that is a matter for her conscience and her God.
> He has in any case been concerned to destroy her confidence
> in her own power, to reduce her self-respect and make her
> willing to lead a dependent and unworthy life.
>
> *Declaration of Sentiments, Seneca Falls 1848*

The Bible and the women's movement

Our Western Christian society has been unsettled by the
changing image of women. However, the churches have been
challenged by it even more painfully, since the document of
their self-understanding, the Bible, contains statements which
negate and defame the autonomy of the woman. For example:

> As in all the churches of the saints, the women should keep
> silence in the churches. For they are not permitted to
> speak, but should be subordinate, as even the law says (I
> Cor.14.34).
>
> Let a woman learn in silence with all submissiveness. I
> permit no woman to teach or to have authority over men;
> she is to keep silent. For Adam was formed first, then Eve;
> and Adam was deceived and became a transgressor. Yet
> woman will be served through bearing children... (I
> Tim.2.11-15).
>
> Drooping hands and weak knees are caused by the wife
> who does not make her husband happy. From a woman sin

had its beginning, and because of her we all die (Sirach 25.23f.).

So far what has been an accepted understanding of culture since the 1920s has found no place in the kind of thinking which is based on such biblical statements. By that I mean the anthropological insights of figures like Margaret Mead,[1] that our biological framework is not enough to determine the 'nature' of the woman and that in fact social influences shape what we regard as 'masculine' and 'feminine'. Margaret Mead and writers like Simone de Beauvoir and Betty Friedan, who have built on these insights, had to remain outside the churches. 'Men's world, women's place' – this old order is still largely the practice of the churches, where it is literally the case that the woman's place is the pew and the man's world is that of church government and theology. This order or disorder is all the more significant in that the churches in fact have a majority of women who are led by a minority group (at least 65% of those who go to church are women). What begins in society from numerous other presuppositions is here distorted even more and in addition is given religious credentials. So the women's movements accuse the churches of being those most responsible for the oppression of women. For August Bebel[2] and Simone de Beauvoir[3] the Bible, and especially the letters of Paul with their principle of the subordination of women, are the main instrument of this oppression. The American Elizabeth Gould Davis[4] warns the churches that they should forgive woman their sins, just as they have also forgiven Jews their crime.

On the other hand there are women who from the beginning of the women's movements in the last century appealed to their rights and understood themselves as complete individuals on the basis of Christianity and found their motivations there. Louise Otto-Peters, the leading light of the German women's movement, did not want to count herself among the 'emancipated' but was proud to be a successor of that 'noble virgin of

Bethany of whom the shining example of all humanity says, Mary has chosen the better part'.[5] Helene Lange spoke of the 'feminism' which will gain the victory 'over the giants and titans of world history' and which she found in the Gospels and in Jesus of Nazareth in the idea of making 'the moral standard the measure of things'.[6] In England Josephine Butler, who brought into being the European movement for the abolition of prostitution, appealed for initiatives from women 'to the book of the Bible that is accessible to all'.[7] A version of the Bible revised by one of the leaders of the American women's movement, Elizabeth Cady Stanton, contributed to the enlightenment of American women.

The women's movement and Christianity have constantly come into contact. Where are the common foundations and where are the differences? In the meantime the international women's movement has produced theological research which gives us new viewpoints and insights. The church and the women's movement therefore often look like two hostile sisters who have forgotten their common origins. In the following sections I want to make clear the connection between the two and also show the conditions under which the hostility between them developed.

The Jesus movement

We now know that the Jesus movement was a non-ascetical, charismatic, itinerant movement. Women and men followed the itinerant preacher Jesus who proclaimed the imminent dawn of the kingdom of God, a social and personal revolution in all values. But this movement was not a movement of renunciation and repentance like that of John the Baptist, nor a male sect like that of Qumran. We know from the stories that were handed down about Jesus that he enjoyed festivals, that he spoke to a great variety of marginal groups and above all dealt with women in an absolute partnership. To the amazement and scandal even of his closest male friends he

79

actually preferred them, and we may infer from the stories handed down to us that he was not cross with any woman (Hanna Wolff).[8] In the early communities which formed after his death stories were handed down which reflect this openness and this social revolution.

Two things are worth noting in these stories.

1. Jesus frees women from traditional social roles, from family associations. He addresses them as individuals and makes them independent individuals. In following him Joanna presumably left her husband, the finance minister at the court of King Herod, and on Easter morning was by the tomb of the 'enemy of the state' (Luke 8.3; 24.10). The mother of the sons of Zebedee did not flee at Jesus' arrest, as did her sons, but stood by the cross – a distinct individual on the basis of her own decision (Matt.26.56; 27.55).[9] In our family-orientated churches we have forgotten that the gospel first of all makes people individuals and gives them courage to become individuals, men and women.

2. Jesus breaks the tabus which surrounded women in the East. He accepts them in all their bodily existence as complete people, though their bodies were regarded as being weak, impure, incapable of being involved in the cult. He heals the woman with a haemorrhage, who was cultically and socially impure and isolated because of her bleeding (Mark 5.25ff.). He even touched sick women: Peter's mother-in-law (Mark 1.30) and Jairus' daughter (Mark 5.41).[10] In one manuscript (Luke 23.2) he is accused of having led women and children astray. In our belief in redemption, which is limited to soul and spirit, we have forgotten what a physical, bodily, tender, indeed erotic dimension the liberation of Jesus has.

Morever, women were the only ones who did not flee at his arrest. They were also the only friends to stand under his cross; they went to the tomb and were the first witnesses of the resurrection. They are regarded today as the real bearers of the tradition of the death and resurrection of Jesus.

This preferential role is reflected in some early communities

with charismatic organization. Women had a function in
leading the community; they were apostles and bishops. One
contemporary describes in a mocking way how women
apportioned offices in the Christian communities. Women in
the New Testament whom we all know – Mary Magdalene,
wrongly known as a great sinner; Martha, only known as a
faithful housewife – were such women who acted as leaders.
In a wide variety of cultures in antiquity women played a
prominent role and their capabilities were discovered. They
succeeded in gaining great independence and recognition as
independent businesswomen. But this never had a lasting
social effect. We must agree with Hanna Wolff when she
says that Jesus was the first man who 'broke through the
androcentricism of the ancient world'.[11] In his person and in
his history the traditional animosity against women and the
discrimination which arose from it seem to have been transcended. Was Jesus a feminist?[12] Did he integrate so many
male and female modes of behaviour in his person that he
could be understood as the mature integrated man (Hanna
Wolff)? We shall come back to the person of Jesus again later.
At least he made history – including women's history. This
called forth movements which extend from antiquity to the
present. The great founders of religion at all times were
friendly to women, but great women's movements which
changed society arose only in the context of Western
Christianity.

However, now a difficulty arises and we can rightly ask: how
did such integrated communities come to have a command for
silence, that women should be silent in the community? How
did it come about that after such beginnings we could be told
that women sinned first and are therefore in special need of
redemption? Does this not go directly against what we now
know about Jesus and the women in the Gospels and the early
church? The gospel has been handed down to us through the
New Testament in a patriarchal form. It has been androcentr-
ically edited in the Bible, i.e. with men as the centre. It has

been patriarchally received in Western tradition and even now it is translated, interpreted and preached in a patriarchal way.

A few examples should make this clear.

Patriarchal redaction

The New Testament has been brought together from different sources, stories, reports and letters. The authors of the parts known to us are male, and in the stories about Jesus the twelve male disciples apparently play the decisive role. Its canonical form comes from a time in which the church had adapted itself to patriarchal forms of society and presented the gospel in this patriarchal form. However, behind it we can recognize the strata which still contain the original traditions. Contemporary New Testament scholarship shows that the New Testament traditions about women only appear in the Bible like the tip of an iceberg.[13] But this tip, too, is still clearly recognizable. What was under it must have been bigger, more powerful and – if we think in terms of the iceberg simile – more dangerous than we now suspect. Documents seem to have disappeared and been destroyed, names deleted or changed. We can only guess at the processes which were involved here.

For example, the tradition of the twelve disciples is constantly cited as evidence of the original masculinity of the church of Jesus Christ. For the Catholic church this is an official doctrine. However, the Twelve also play a decisive role for many other churches. They are regarded as the real disciples, successors and bearers of tradition. But if we look closer we discover quite a different tradition in the earliest Gospel, the Gospel of Mark: the real followers of Jesus are the women, for they serve Jesus, just as Jesus has come to serve and to give his life for others. They are the real sharers in the messianic secret, and guess in advance at his death and its significance. And later they become the real bearers of the tradition of his death and resurrection.[14] We shall come back to that later in more detail. Over against that the role of the Twelve is as negative as can be: they do not appear in the discipleship of serving, they are in love with success, they do not understand Jesus and want to prevent his passion. It is clear that the Twelve – as representatives of a church adapted to patriarchal conditions and as a stylized embodiment of the twelve tribes of Israel – have introduced a bias into these original stories. In the later Gospels, above all in Luke, the role of the Twelve was then established as that of an élite celibate group, and clear deletions were made from the women's tradition.

Paul's famous command that women should keep silent is another example of the patriarchal redaction of the Bible. 'Let women keep silent in church.' This statement occurs in I Corinthians (I Cor.14.34f.) and its fatal influence is well known. But it does not seem to come from Paul himself, since in Paul we find the revolutionary statement from an early Christian baptismal confession that in Christ there are neither Jews nor Greeks, neither servant nor free, neither man nor woman (Gal.3.28). A third of his collaborators were women, probably with just the same rights as the men. And if Paul was perhaps no special supporter of women, the command to silence goes against his theology and the practice in the community of his time. It occurs again e.g. in I Timothy (2.12f.), a letter from the late period, when the bishop had to be male and the woman silent. From this letter, which does not derive from Paul, but is attributed to him, this saying found its way into I Corinthians as an insertion.[15] In this way a patriarchal church structure was projected back into an early church structure of equality.

If we go back behind this redaction we read the stories of Jesus and the women with new eyes; we note the conduct of the women, and then we find them tough, wise debaters, full of imagination and self-awareness, who break with convention and emancipate themselves from old family roles. Women are not primarily defined in the New Testament narratives by family roles but by their calling and their own actions. But in the course of the patriarchalizing of church structures they

83

were again made into housewives obedient to their husbands.[16] They were incorporated into the family and they perhaps experienced the liberation which Jesus had brought from the fact that their husbands treated them better.

From now on the image of the Christian *paterfamilias* is inseparable from the Christian religion. He is the head of the family, to whom wife and children are subordinate, a loving patriarch of whom society has expectations. The woman is forced back into the role of mother without being able also to understand herself in the community in terms of her charismatic functions.

Patriarchal reception

The second misfortune came about when the Bible, which had already undergone patriarchal editing, was now again received in a patriarchal way in Western tradition. This happened in the second half of the first millennium, when the Christian West developed, the persecuted church became a state church and papacy and hierarchy came into being. Much that in the first centuries of Christian life was still charismatic, colourful, varied and lively, was now increasingly codified and rationalized. I would like to demonstrate this development by means of a living women's tradition which can still be recognized in the Bible, about Mary Magdalene.[17]

The New Testament says of her that she was healed of an epileptic illness and followed Jesus. She was the leader of the group of women and was the first to have the task of proclaiming the resurrection of Christ to the disciples. Still in the first centuries and even later in the Eastern churches she is the chaste friend of Jesus and is regarded by many church fathers as the apostle of all apostles. On a mediaeval altar wing she even nominates a bishop (see the plate on p. 12). However, at an early stage a successful patriarchal falsification of history began which only ended with the reform of the Roman breviaries in the 1970s: the figure of Mary Magdalene (Luke

8.3) was confused with that of the woman who was a sinner (Luke 7.36ff.). She became the prototype of sensuality and sexual sin, a development which, as Karl Künste says, was particularly encouraged by Augustine, as he himself was caught 'in the bonds of sensuality'.[18] At this time the West primarily located sin in the body and sexuality, and projected its theological problems on to a woman. The Magdalene tradition has flourished down to the present day in all the churches, in literature and in graphic art, and many theologians even now regard Mary Magdalene as the great sinner (see the plate on p.76). The development of hierarchy, the codification and rationalizaton of the content of faith was matched by a separation of the spheres of emotion and the senses, leading to an underestimation of them and finally an interpretation of them as temptation and sin. And women became the victims.

For his time Augustine put this very aptly: for him emotionalism is flesh, rationality spirit; the woman is the embodiment of the flesh, the man the embodiment of the spirit, and the relationship between the two reflects the Christian world order:

> Where the flesh rules and the spirit serves, the house is in disorder. What is worse than a house where the woman has rule over the man? However, a house is right where the man commands and the woman obeys. So man is right where the spirit rules and the flesh serves.[19]

In this hierarchical order man is the supreme form of human life. In mediaeval church doctrine woman is even said not to be in the image of God: *mulier non est gloria et imago Dei* (Thomas Aquinas), and she is regarded as an incomplete man (*vir imperfectus*).[20] Confronted with the women's movements which developed in the eleventh and twelfth century the church clearly moved over to misogyny. In the face of the new movements of the Cathari and the Waldensians, among whom women had the right to preach and sometimes to administer the sacraments, the male priesthood was defended with all available means: the woman was accused of cultic impurity as she had been in Judaism. Only the male was immediate to God (Huggicio); he was the direct image of God. The mediaeval persecution of witches was then simply a consequence of church teaching.

We must constantly remind ourselves that such perversions as those of Thomas Aquinas were no longer just proclaimed from teaching chairs, and that the woman was still regarded as an irrational, seductive being.

One can still sometimes find the relics of such patriarchal superiority even in our time, as e.g. when in 1940 the then leader of National Women's Aid, Adolf Brandmeyer, preached to women: 'Christ frees you mothers from your impulses and calls you as joyful, obedient maidens in his community...'[21]

Adolf Schlatter, the well-known theologian, was afraid of having a woman in the pulpit because he feared sexual excitement among the congregation.

> But never do away with the special characteristics of the congregation peculiar to their sexes. That first of all means that they are to be excluded from the public administration of the religious word, because in the communication of the divine message to men only its content should have an effect, and not feminine charm at the same time. Here one should think not only of the possibility that impure desires might arise but also that the quite natural attraction of the form and voice of the woman which is her constant accompaniment is not the way by which the attestation of faith arouses faith in us.[22]

Even now, most Christians regard Mary Magdalene as the great sinner, though no male equivalent has appeared. We know from psychology of the deep-seated significance of images – combined with concepts – on human consciousness. The woman who is sexualized, a slave to desires, weakness and sin, does not belong in the gospel but in its patriarchal alienation. The woman belongs in the gospel which knows that she is accepted with all of her existence.

Patriarchal interpretation and translation

A third patriarchal alienation of the gospel takes place day by day in our church praxis. Women are hardly still discriminated against as 'Eve', but they are constantly reminded of their 'otherness'. On the one hand an appeal is made to their capacity for surrender, their motherliness, the strength of their feelings, their power of love, which are in contrast to the harshness of the rest of the world – in other words, women are emotionalized. If one reads commentaries on particular narratives about women in the New Testament, one very soon detects the sort of ideal of woman the theologian has. Usually it is the ideal of the modest woman who is restrained, always open and adaptable. By contrast loudness, eloquence, a will of one's own, are not desired and quickly disqualified.

This emotionalizing corresponds above all to the needs of the industrial age. In the face of technology feeling is sought as a supplement, and spontaneity in the face of reason. As in the Middle Ages, when the repressed sexuality in woman was rediscovered, so now people project their unfulfilled wishes for an emotional world on the woman. And again the woman is stereotyped, made the object of others' needs and robbed of her self-determination.

The same emotionalizing and stereotyping in roles which are apparently sexually conditioned is also evident in our biblical narratives. As an example I would like to mention the beginning of Rom.16. There (v.1) Paul commends to the community a woman called Phoebe whom he describes as *diakonos* and *prostatis*. Since the translators render the word *diakonos* in the connection with masculine names as 'helper' or 'deacon', Phoebe becomes for them a 'deaconess' (Revised Standard Version), an 'auxiliary' (*The Jerome Biblical*

Commentary),[23] a 'helper' (*A New Catholic Commentary on Holy Scripture*)[24] or simply a 'servant' (Revised Version). The fact that 'deacon of the church of Cenchreae' denotes a position of leadership does not emerge from this.

The word *prostatis* is rendered as 'helper' or as a verb, 'look after', i.e. typical functions of a woman. Elisabeth Schüssler-Fiorenza has shown that in Jewish terminology *prostatis*, which does not occur elsewhere in the New Testament, has the meaning leader, president, governor. As a verb (I Tim.3.4f.; 5.17) it denotes the service of bishops, deacons and elders.[25] So Phoebe must have been a person in authority functioning as a leader.

Here Paul mentions a married couple, Prisca and Aquila (v.3). However, our translations of the Bible, e.g. the Good News Version, have often, in accordance with our social order, put the husband Aquila in first place and always reduced Prisca to Priscilla, though according to the NT the woman was probably more significant. Finally, Paul writes of two apostles, Andronicus and Junias (v.7), who in our Bibles are regarded as men. However, we now know that Junias was a female apostle by the name of Junia. But this did not fit the Christian picture of the world, so she was made into a man.[26]

In such types of exegesis the 'serving' which is mentioned in connection with the women and Jesus finally loses its original character as established by Jesus. The serving of the women which sets them on the same level as Jesus becomes the friendly 'lend assistance' (Luther Bible), the good bourgeois 'caring' and 'looking after' (Good News) or social 'support' (United Bible). This completes the process of making the group of women into housewives and removes the dynamite that was among them.

Diaconia – service – is a basic Christian task. It is not something that is specific to one sex. Jesus the man came to serve and give his life. But serving and leading were quickly torn apart and the women were left with service as their finest adornment and basic task, apparently in accordance with their feeling about the world.

From this patriarchal tradition we carry around with us a twofold burden. First there is an idea of order and lordship which assigns the woman particular – allegedly feminine – functions and prevents democratic, charismatic developments even in the sphere of the family. And secondly, there is an alienation from and hostility to the body which still makes it difficult for us to experience ourselves as whole people with body, soul and spirit, to develop male and female possibilities and to accept our bodies with all our suppressed wishes, desires and dreams.

We must learn a new way of dealing with the Bible which developed in favour of the church tradition at the expense of the woman: one which is existential, corporeal and critical.

Wisdom enthroned with seven books and a flowering sceptre, eleventh-century Bible manuscript, Paris

6

GOD, OUR MOTHER

Thus I will always remain a stubborn protester against the unreasonable Protestantism which in the heights in the kingdom of God accepts only one Son, but no mother and sister. I think that women in particular should stick out their necks like heroes against such a Protestantism and protest against a concern to reduce their sex to an insignificant nothingness in the kingdom of God.

J.J. Wirz

Replacement of the Father

In the male-edited Bible with its increasing contempt for women the images of God which are used are predominantly masculine. God is king, judge, warrior, banker. His activities reflect predominantly male actions. He reigns, rules, judges, punishes, rewards, pays. His properties derive from masculine desires for strength, sovereignty, omnipotence. Language and ideas in the Bible and the church have been orientated on the image of the male as the normal case or as the supreme form of human life: being a Christian is chivalry, faith is a battle or duel which ends with honour for the victor. The gospel is to be spread around at top speed. Shield and spear, at that time the weapons of defence and attack, are now almost impossible to think out of the Christian vocabulary. The aggression they unleash only becomes clear when we replace them with images of contemporary armament.

But so far faith in God the Father has been deeply rooted in Christian culture. When people nowadays are asked what belief in God the Father means for them, two elements emerge clearly: becoming a person and security. 'When I say Our Father,' writes the Latin American Bishop Antonio Fragoso, 'the words bring to mind both certainties and challenges.' And in the same way a woman, Irene de Bourbon-Parma, says that she prays the Our Father to a God 'from whom I look for protection, although I know that he wants me, as a human being, to go my own way, in faith'.[1]

But many women today seek more of what their 'psychological matriarchy' urges on them: basic physical rights, i.e. self-determination over their bodies, free sexuality, cosmic ties and solidarity. They have too often experienced becoming a person as paternal spoon-feeding and security.

The image of God as Father had been useful for forming personality in a patriarchal society. In a hierarchy it offered protection and privacy, trust and security. For a changing society which is apparently fatherless and has undergone a process of internalizing patriarchal laws, images and ideas are needed to replace the restrictive patriarchal morality which puts women in their place.

Catharina Halkes still sees these patriarchalistic restrictions in her Catholic view of the church and even attaches to it the character of revelation:

> This pattern of man as powerful and woman as subject, which is so clearly symbolized in the image of God the Father, is so deeply rooted in our thinking and imagination that it is experienced as divine revelation itself and therefore as unchangeable. That explains why women are deprived of the opportunity to give meaning to themselves personally, physically and sexually and why they are prevented from having any official or sacramental responsibility in the church or the liturgy. It also explains why the church's teaching about sexuality and the family is dualistic and abstract.[2]

As soon as depth psychology emerged in the 1920s, women began to detect the one-dimensional character of the Christian male image of God. It was clear at the time that masculinity was connected with understanding, victory, light. That was abundantly evident in the language and conceptuality of the church. However, the dark, emotional and undervalued realms found no place there. The name 'Lord', Dora Lent wrote at the time, cuts right through the middle of everything, 'summons only the spirit, the male half' and silences God's womanhood.[3] What to my mind is the first modern prayer in the German language to meet the need for a whole God, 'Our Father-Mother in heaven', was written at the time by a woman who because of insights gained from depth psychology did not want to go on separating light and darkness, life and death, woman and man.[4]

Hardly anything has changed today in this solar, masculine preponderance. As Christa Mulack observes,

theology still fails to see that it has furthered, not the worship of God but that of a patriarchal idol, thus as it were offending against part of the tradition which underlies its discourses, in which man and woman are depicted as human and as the image of God only in their togetherness. Far too little attention is paid to this connection in Judaism and Christianity. Both preferred as their God the absolutized male will and still do not dare to ask behind the patriarchs who were given grace by God...[5]

The search for true mothers

The knowledge and awareness in the second women's movement in the 1970s of living in a patriarchal society and being condemned as a woman to powerlessness and non-identity has intensified the search for God the mother. For now more than a psychological experience of wholeness is at stake. The question is how women who are discriminated against in every aspect of their existence can achieve power out of powerlessness, not the patriarchal power of self-assertion and ruthlessness, but a more friendly power which could also produce a new society. The concern now is with the 'dark' side of all society and its fundamental questioning by women.

The search for God the mother, for God as woman, is the search for true mothers who allow this cosmic breadth and do not shut off spheres of life from their daughters by restrictive laws. The search for God as wife and mother goes beyond our damaged conceptions of mothers in which anxiety about and dependence on the all-devouring mother played a decisive role. Such universal mothers, representing nature and wisdom, should not be dependent on male needs and therefore should not require their children to be so dependent but accept them and love them unconditionally. The search for female conceptions of God is the search for total conceptions of life which point beyond our patriarchal limitations and constrictions.

Some attempts should be mentioned here.

Since for Mary Daly the dominant understanding of being banishes women to non-being, the important thing in her view is to create a new being on the periphery of non-being and boldly counter non-being. In a woman's own being she sees the divine spark which is no longer to be spoken of anthropomorphically but gynomorphically, in female pictures. In her there is experience of the goddess, the being that loves life, the confirmation of the being of women and nature.

Although Christianity has forced on Mary a saccharine quality of purity, Daly still sees in her something of the manifestation of the transcendence of the great mother which could not be destroyed. Detached from the church context 'Mary rising' still has something to say. The great mother, psychologized in this way, now celebrates resurrection in the sisterhood of the anti-church.[6]

The goddess and her anthropological function for women today becomes more tangible in Heide Göttner-Abendroth. Cast out by the Protestant work ethic and the innermost image of God, by means of the Catholic myth she found Mary, 'behind whose beautiful mythological veil, however, she comes up against harsh, inexorable dogma', the image of the goddess and her hero. She thinks that she can find matriarchal culture and society again in it. The goddess and her hero were the two cosmic powers and, as priestess and king, also the two social powers. They also represent the two psychological powers in humanity: the feminine principle as the divine, the power for integration, and the male principle as the heroic, the capacity for integrity. Instead of the 'faded' conceptions of *animus* and *anima* invented by male psychology (C.G.Jung), the images of the goddess and her hero depict the capacities for creativity and self-sacrifice which can be discovered in any human being. They depict totality on the basis of the female primal principle.[7]

In her quest to free herself from her own restrictive mother, 'a little Demeter' bought cheaply in Florence has helped Ursa Krattiger to find a way to the great goddess, the great mother, the womb of all things: Demeter is a divine image of primal growth, an archetype, of which is it is said in the Gospel of Thomas: 'My physical mother bore me, but my true mother gave me life.' All maternal conflicts can now be buried, the new birth has begun, 'Eternal mother be praised, be glorified.'[8]

The contemporary cultivation of the feminine sometimes issues in demands to recognize child-bearing again as a divine activity. This seems more fascist that forward-looking to those who had experience of the Third Reich. Other proposals – corresponding to depth-psychological models of the consciousness which is embedded in the unconscious for making the male an auxiliary function of the female – can hardly be of much use for human relationships and social changes as they simply represent the mirror-image of wrong relationships: here the great mother again takes on totalitarian features, similarities to the great Father whom women wanted to leave behind.

Are there in the Christian tradition, which played a decisive role in the cult of the father, and which despite everything is the tradition of freedom, images of God which make possible new total conceptions of life?

95

Wisdom

'God is Father, but to a much greater degree he is also Mother.' That was the reaction to questions put by women some years ago from the then supreme head of the Catholic church. Every theological student learns that in Hebrew the mercy of God is called *rechem*, mother's love. Anyone who has grown up in the Protestant church will have had a wealth of pictures of God as mother from the hymns of Paul Gerhard; for example, 'With mother's hands he leads his children on.' The basis for these images is the Old Testament, where God's action towards Israel, his faithfulness and his care, are often depicted in images of motherly love: 'Can a wife forget her child or a mother her son?' And Yahweh the warrior, who goes to battle for his people, is transformed into a woman: 'Now I will cry out like a woman in travail' (Isa.42.13f.).

But, many women ask today, is not this in the end the old male God who has taken on a few feminine characteristics? Does he not remain essentially male? Have not the fertility goddesses been exterminated in his name and has he not for centuries served to stabilize patriarchal society? Is not ultimately even the androgynous God, the god with male and female properties, a male God to whom female properties have been added? Is this not an invention of male theology which detects its deficiency but would never accept a gynaeco-centric picutre of God (one orientated upon women)? In the Council of Toledo in 675 God was even said to have a uterus from which he bore his Son, but this organ which he was given in no way changed his maleness.[9]

More important than references to the maternal properties of God is the rediscovery of the figure of wisdom in the Old Testament. She is not androgynous (male-female). She is female (see the plate on p.90). She is almost like a second person of God present at the work of creation: she 'played before him always'(Prov.8.30).

She is described as the daughter of God, his companion,

and is called sister, wife, mother, beloved and teacher. She leads along new ways, she is the preacher and master-workman of all things.She seeks people, finds them on the way and invites them to eat. She offers life, rest, knowledge and healing to those who accept her and makes them friends of God. In turn she is sought, beloved but also rejected. However, anyone who misses her comes to grief. Those who hate her are necrophilic (love death, Prov.8.36). But those who follow her are preserved from evil.

In contrast to many other conceptions of God, to begin with there is no question of compulsion. She is 'a spotless mirror of the working of God, and an image of his goodness'. She is undivided, whole, 'though she is only one, she can do all things' (Wisdom 7.27). Even evil can do nothing against her. However, no penalties, no ideas of retribution or reward are associated with her and her invitation or repudiation. She is good, goodness, and makes the one who accepts her invitation good, understanding and rich (cf. Prov.8ff.; Sirach 1; Wisdom 7ff.).

Underlying this imposing figure of wisdom are relics of a cult of female deities in the ancient Near East. In these cults goddesses were worshipped as the givers of life, as creators and redeemers. They represented both social justice and harmony with nature. And they were an independent women's tradition, even if they were integrated into the Jewish tradition. From the third century BC onwards the figure of wisdom was revered in Jewish wisdom theology – probably above all under Egyptian influence.[10]

The 'goddess' wisdom also reaches out into the New Testament. Elisabeth Schüssler-Fiorenza has shown that the all-embracing unconditional love of God proclaimed by Jesus is to be understood against the background of the wisdom tradition. It governs the cosmic solidarity which comes from God, who makes his/her sun shine on the good and evil and makes the rain fall on the just and the unjust. It brings social equality which is experienced in the table-fellowship of Jesus with tax-gatherers, sinners, outsiders and prostitutes. Elements of goddess language are used in the language of wisdom theology in order to demonstrate the all-embracing matriarchal love of God. 'The divine Sophia is Israel's God in the language and form of the goddess' (Elisabeth Schüssler-Fiorenza).

Investigations by Felix Christ show that later Jesus himself was seen as Sophia, who is rejected and repudiated, and that the earliest christology was sophialogy.[11] However, only remnants of this christology are still to be found in the New Testament. The dominant element in theological and Christian awareness was that Christ is the Word, the Logos. The Logos christology became predominant. But the Logos is only the male form of wisdom. The wisdom tradition that we are now rediscovering in a surprisingly multiple form was left to marginal Christian groups, heretics and mystics. In the first Christian centuries it was the central message of many communities which were well disposed towards women. In the Middle Ages it formed part of the confession of faith of Julian of Norwich. It stamped the mysticism of the seventeenth century and at a time of male dominance, rationality and exclusiveness it preserved the breadth, comprehensibility and openness of Christian love – for both women and men.

Shekinah and Holy Spirit

From the beginning of our era, in rabbinic mysticism the place of wisdom is taken by another form of the feminine presence of God, the Shekinah. The celebration of the sabbath was regarded as the mystical marriage of God with his Shekinah which anticipated the final reunion of God with creation. The Shekinah is something like the cosmic, reconciling, earthly side of God which accompanies Israel into exile, whereas God has hidden himself in anger.[12]

The Holy Spirit (and in German it can take the feminine form, Heilige Geistin), is still closely connected with femininity

and women's tradition. *ruach* – spirit is feminine in Hebrew
and then became neuter, *pneuma* in Greek; finally it became
the Latin masculine *Spiritus*, the Western Holy Spirit.[13]
Despite this Western patriarchalization the Spirit was often
thought to be feminine. For example in the Urschalling depiction of the Trinity the third person of the Trinity is a woman.
The dove, the symbol of the Spirit, still recalls its feminine
origins.

Above all in the Eastern church the old matriarchal
traditions survived. Simeon of Mesopotamia called the Spirit
'our heavenly mother' in the Homilies which were re-edited by
Gottfried Arnold.[14] Pietism took up this notion and Zinzendorf
made it binding on the Communities of Brethren: at the
foundation of the first American community of brothers and
sisters in Pennsylvania he spoke of 'the Holy Spirit's office as
mother', but later regretted that this office of mother had not
become a reality in his church: 'It has become a matter of
disorder that the office of the Holy Spirit as mother has not
been disclosed through a sister but through me among the
sisters.'[15]

Since developments in the main traditions of Christianity
got in the way of thinking of the feminine in connection with
God, the Western doctrine of the Trinity developed completely
in accordance with a patriarchal model. However, the excep-
tions and deviations from the norm should again make us
aware of the permeability of this system. In mysticism, the
revivalist movement and pietism, old traditions again broke
through, even if the the power that shaped the traditions was
male, and the female tended to be on the receiving end.

The non-patriarchal Father

The critical question is whether women today are not so
enthusiastic over so many new discoveries about the femininity
of God, above all through the figure of Sophia, that they
overlook the fact that Jesus spoke of God the Father and that

he taught his female and male disciples the 'Our Father'. No note is taken here of the fact that the real, original form of address used by Jesus was not Father, but Abba. Joachim Jeremias says of this word:

> To the Jewish mind it would have been disrespectful and therefore inconceivable to address God with this familiar word. For Jesus to venture to take this step was something new and unheard-of. He spoke to God like a child to its father, simply, inwardly, confidently.[16]

So Abba is an intimate word and thus an affront to any patriarchal structure. It shows no respect and makes God familiar and near. However, only Mark has preserved this direct familiarity between father and child; in the later Gospels the relationship between the two is already characterized by obedience. 'To do the will of God' in Mark is still a matter of being in tune with the community of God, something which also comes about through communion with sisters and brothers. This traumatic word 'obedience' is only developed fully in Pauline theology. In Mark we can detect nothing of this structure of obedience which was later to have a fatal effect, and which entered Christianity with hierarchical and patriarchal thought. Thus from the perspective of the psychology of religion, Christa Mulack can say of this original, non-patriarchal use by Jesus of the term Abba: 'The Father has become one with the Great Mother: he realizes her, she has entered into him and realizes herself through him, so that the two can no longer be distinguished.'[17]

Gerhard Lohfink's comment on Jesus' understanding of the Father shows a similar break with the current image of Jesus.[18] Jesus calls people out of family ties, himself violates family duties, in a way which according to Old Testament law calls for the death penalty. 'He who does the will of God is my mother, my brother, my sister.' These are the words he uses to describe the new community. Those who follow him and have left all family ties – father, mother, children – behind them will rediscover in the new community everything that they have left behind: 'house and brothers and sisters and mothers and children and fields...' However, remarkably there is no mention of fathers that they will rediscover (Mark 10.29,30). The new community is a community of wives and mothers, but it is free from paternal structures, even if it came into being in the environs of the man Jesus. According to Elisabeth Schüssler-Fiorenza, 'Call no one father, for you have one Father' must therefore have been what Jesus originally said (Matt.23.9). Here is a challenge to today's churches with their fathers in the faith, fathers in orders, church fathers and Holy Father. As Elisabeth Schüssler-Fiorenza puts it, 'The Father God of Jesus makes possible the sisterliness of men by challenging the right of all fathers and all patriarchy to exist.' Underneath the upper stratum of the New Testament, which seems to us to be so male, with its conflict between Father and Son, and the twelve male disciples, we can see a stratum in which a non-patriarchal community is given the right to exist by a non-patriarchal God. But church history shows that this breakthrough was not maintained and that is already evident from the New Testament. It is important today to uncover the roots again and see behind the patriarchal language and structure of the tradition the non-patriarchal heritage which has become obscured.

However, what remain in the centre of theological interest are not the hidden conceptions of Jesus about Sophia God, but the ideas he expressed about God the Father. They shaped the fate of church and theology. Here the theologians began with their basic interest in male models. These conceptions found their way into the Bible. The conflict between Father and Son was reflected in the doctrine of the Trinity and ethics. Faith in God the Father was significantly and usefully turned into the formation of personality in a patriarchal society.

But the God whom Jesus proclaimed is rooted in the matriarchal Sophia tradition. Jesus' way of addressing God as Abba and the sisterly, non-patriarchal social order which he depicts are in accord with this picture of God. However, these matriarchal beginnings were absorbed by patriarchal society and remained a living potential only in marginal Christian traditions, which offered self-awareness, wisdom and survival above all to women.

The images of God in the Bible have more possibilities for female identification than is generally assumed. They were and are capable of being interpreted in non-patriarchal ways. They were and are open for theophantasy. This is above all evident, however, in the conceptions of the sub-culture.

Kether, Hokmah and Binah – three feminine images of the Trinity. Didactic tablet of Princess Antonia, 1673, Bad Teinach

7

MATRIARCHAL SUB-CULTURE

> Had women, in the background position assigned to them, not
> retained an emotional criterion for the position of human beings
> in the world and for the principles of a humane society, the
> escapades of male megalomania would have had to end in
> general disaster.
>
> *Horst Eberhard Richter*

The underside of history

If we arc to get a total insight into the Christian women's
tradition it is important to incorporate the unwritten history
of women. This underside of history is still unknown and the
whole of its scope has still to be discovered. Were there other
conceptions of woman, God and salvation than those in the
patriarchal tradition with which we are familiar?

The Christian-Jewish religion was from the very beginning
surrounded by matriarchal or partially matriarchal religions.
Faith in Yahweh had developed and taken shape with the
incursion of patriarchal northern tribes into the Mediterranean, which still had a matriarchal stamp. 'In the second
millennium the patriarchal worshippers of the Father God had
poured into almost all the goddess-worshipping civilizations,
from the Indus Valley in the east through Mesopotamia and
Asia Minor to early Europe in the west... Presumably Egypt
was the only country not to be conquered by the patriarchal
Indo-Europeans.'[1] The old world was replaced by the patriarchal world with its other symbols and other values. Two
completely different concepts made contact.

The old religion, however, seems to have gone on flourishing among the people for a long time. The protests of the prophets against the fertility cults bear witness to a long, tough battle between the new patriarchal religion and the old matriarchal one. The vehicles of this cult were presumably women, some of whom came from the subject population (cf. Deut.21.10-14) who preserved *their* conceptions of life, of God and of salvation.

In Europe in the early Middle Ages Christianity then met up again with strongly matriarchal Celtic religious feeling, which can be traced in Ireland and southern France right down to the late Middle Ages. So there were periods of specific contact between Christianity and matriarchal cultures. Heide Göttner-Abendroth has demonstrated a matriarchal opposition as late as the mediaeval epics.[2] Is there also a corresponding matriarchal opposition in the Christian religion and its forms of expression?

In my view a variety of matriarchal elements found their way into the Jewish-Christian religion. However, we must learn to distinguish and discover these elements. We must above all find new criteria for our theological thought and our theological research.

First of all it should be noted that the Jewish-Christian religion is a religion which is fixed in writing. Writing, education, science, religion in a patriarchy is above all in the hands of males. The Jewish-Christian religion is one which was written down by men, who presumably introduced the perspectives and interests of the ruling class. Just as theology so far has developed a wrong or inadequate picture of women and their circumstances, or even no picture at all, so we must also regard the written records of Jewish-Christian faith – Old Testament, New Testament, canon law, dogmatics – as one-sided and inadequate sources. Matriarchal pictures or ways of thinking have come in only unconsciously or in a marginal way. Even in the social context Ernst Bloch has raised the critical question whether the Bible is not made a 'theocratic common denominator' so that it is difficult to see the subversive traditions of Judaism.[3] We can also conjecture today a patriarchal common denominator to which much has fallen victim.

Unwritten traditions

Written religion is often overvalued. Fascinated by the knowledge that has been newly disclosed to them, women too have often seen it as the only source of religion and thus fallen victim to masculine, inculcated patterns of behaviour. Alongside written religion there is a lived religion which often looks amazingly different. For example the patriarchalizing of the Holy Spirit in writing has not reached the levels of popular piety and popular belief. The Russian Margarita Voloshin reports that in her country the mother earth is identical in popular belief with the mother of God, with Sophia. 'The Holy Spirit lives in the earth,' an old Russian proverb has it, or: 'You should not lie, the earth hears it.' Here Wisdom, Spirit and the Great Mother are still cosmic powers which are not incorporated under any patriarchal common denominator.[4]

However, this lived religion is much more difficult to comprehend than written religion, and so far it has hardly been taken note of in theology. Nevertheless, the histories of piety, culture and art are important areas from which religion can be reconstructed. As Helgard Balz-Cochois writes in an investigation on Hosea,

> The written theology of Hosea has survived and created a history of tradition... But is the experiential truth of the people and of Gomer less true and real only because it is vanished and gone, remains unwritten and therefore has no effect on history? Perhaps here one should play off, as a corrective, a feeling related to the present and to experience against a historicization of the concept of truth and reality... Tradition is not just taught and read, it is also experienced, and this is the case above all in illiterate cultural circles.[5]

If we are to investigate the whole reality of religious life and not just the half which finds expression in writing, we should learn to investigate cult, art and documents of piety.

In addition to the fixation of religion in writing and its expression in art and in the cult there is also narrative tradition, though this is harder to comprehend. Many people have had their faith passed on to them through a narrative tradition which is often in amazing contrast to the official religion that is fixed in writing. For example the narrative tradition can be found in mediaeval legends in which biblical and pagan notions are developed further in an imaginative and unconventional way. The narrative tradition often also reflects the tradition of the mothers, their own images and conceptions. We find it, for example, where mothers did not tell their children of a Lord God and a man Jesus, but commmunicated their own freedom and identity with their own experience of God.

I would like to demonstrate this by means of an example which brings us down to the present: my first experience of Jesus was that he is feminine. (Perhaps this is the reason why I never had existential problems over Jesus as a man.) My mother had always talked to me about the Christ child, whom I imagined as a creature of light with a white garment and long shining hair. All the later images of Jesus could not overshadow or overlay this original picture. If we investigate the Christ child we come upon romantic bourgeois Christmas poems. Behind them, however, through contemporary research into myths and folk-tales, including feminist research, another dimension opens up: the Christ child is the pre-Christian relic of the Germanic conceptions of Freia or Frau Holle,[6] who visits the children in winter.

So although my mother never came to know the Goddess in the patriarchal Prussian manse where her parents lived, she brought me the gospel in her own images which are friendly to women, images with which both she and her daughter could identify.

This narrative tradition which existed in many forms, the tradition of wives and mothers, is living proof of a matriarchal sub-culture which helped women to survive in patriarchal Christianity.

If we investigate religion from such total perspectives we come closer to the reality of religious life, the popular reality and above all women's reality. A sub-culture opens up which can be compared with the dominant culture and in which matriarchal elements emerge, are preserved and handed down further.

Woman and serpent

It can be demonstrated from the symbolism of the serpent or dragon how an old and at the same time alternative conception of salvation infiltrated the current patriarchal conception.

Images and dreams of serpents and dragons belong, for members of a patriarchal culture, to the sphere of the imagination, though they also fill us with anxiety and abhorrence.[7] Moreover as Christians we have the serpent from the story of the Fall and the evil apocalyptic dragon, both of which represent evil, the apostasy of man from God and power hostile to God. But the texts from which these images come are not representative of the Bible as a whole. They are patriarchal strands, alongside which there are also other conceptions, according to which the snake, the old symbol of the goddess, also represented fertility and renewal (see the plate on p.42). For example the Yahwistic story of the flood came into being in polemic at a time when Yahwism was in conflict with Canaanite cults and it made use of the matriarchal serpent, the tree of life, the fruit of paradise and Eve, the old goddess of life, to distinguish itself from the old cult and anathematize it. This move proved successful, seeing that patriarchal Christianity is still orientated on it! However, the patriarchal strands can prevent us seeing how stories about the promise of life from the serpent, lifted up and worshipped, in the Old Testament (Num.21.9) and in the Gospel of John (3.14), contain another tradition: here the serpent is still associated with the matriarchal conception that it represents salvation, life, and renewal. But these are subversive images, practised in cults and groups which still had archaic, undivided conceptions of nature and spirit. In the vision of the end-time in the prophet Isaiah (11.8), the serpent again appears in a de-demonized form: in the peace of those days the child will put its hand in the serpent's hole. Beginning time and end time correspond.

However, the regular image in patriarchal culture was the image of the victory over the dragon and its death, an example of human aggression, evoked by anxiety about the irrational, the cosmic, that which can no longer be controlled. It was a symbol of domination which celebrated the victory finally achieved over the lower, terrifying spheres (cf. the plate on p.28). A mosaic of the emperor Constantine showing him and his sons defeating the dragon was presumably normative for the conceptions and the depiction of the victory of Christ over evil and was followed by the countless pictures of the victory over the dragon in Christian iconography (see below). These are the best demonstration of the tragic connection between Christianity and patriarchy, its dreams, anxieties and aggressions.[8] 'Any patriarchal world is proud of depicting itself placing its foot on the dragon's head.'[9]

In the patriarchal world the dragon, the unconscious, the cosmic seat of the feelings as opposed to the will, control and understanding became dangerous and evil, and in patriarchal Christianity the arch-enemy of humanity. Christianity committed the cardinal mistake in its main traditions of identifying what it thought to be the 'hostile to God' with the old symbol of fertility and the woman and once for all depicting the way in which it saw sin and sexuality as going together.

And yet the matriarchal tradition with its friendly attitude to the cosmos lived on. On a romanesque capital in Rozier, Côtes d'Aurec, in France, a redeemed man can be seen with raised arms, holding in one hand an apple, the symbol of the senses and the totality of the world; alongside him is a serpent coiling itself upwards, which in this upright position is a symbol of belief in redemption.[10] In a portrayal of the crucifixion in an ivory relief from Tongeren (eleventh century), Gaea, the earth, is suckling the snake below under the right side of the cross. Usually, according to the patriarchal model, she would be expected on the left ('negative', cf. p.49), side. But she is on the 'right' side and subordinated to Mary and the church. Both Gaea and Ecclesia have a branch or tree with leaves on in their hand as a sign of fertility, an unusual but original view of the unity of earth, cross, tree of life, serpent and woman.[11]

The forgotten goddess in Christianity

In the south of France in the twelfth century there comes into being an image of Martha taming the dragon, which derives from a legendary development of the resurrection of Lazarus, in which Martha was actively involved. It spread with the help of the women of the Cathari and Waldensians and lasted until the Reformation, sometimes into the Baroque period. We may assume that it was cherished in nunneries, and then developed over a broad stratum of the population. The image, which was almost completely forgotten in Christian iconography, continues to represent the forgotten goddess, the integrated woman, in a Christianity that seems to have become very patriarchal. Presumably a local goddess was fused with the biblical figure.[12] The way in which Martha binds the dragon with her girdle recalls the (matriarchal) mistress of the beasts who has cosmic power. It remained an image in the subculture, although it was also painted by famous mediaeval painters. The image for the higher cultural world became that of George the dragon-killer, because it corresponded to the patriarchal world and its ideas.

In a world in which dragon and snake were reduced to being the 'basic symbols of evil' (Ernst Bloch) instead of embodying wisdom, knowledge and healing as in the matriarchal world, the serpent or dragon was again given living room beside the woman's girdle; and as in the Bible, where it restlessly seeks 'to be present at all subversive areas',[13] here it again assumes its original status and the woman gets back her wholeness and originality. St Margaret is another woman who conquers dragons. Above all in Eastern Europe, she too is often depicted with girdle, cross or holy water, but sometimes also fighting in patriarchal fashion with the spear, for the theme of her legend is her attempt to conquer the devil. So this image is no longer so clearly of matriarchal origin as that of Martha.

At the end of the Middle Ages an Eve was created for a pillar of the cathedral in Rheims who now threw aside all the patriarchal Jewish-Christian traditions: Eve holds in her hands pressed to her heart a small dragon which has in its open mouth an apple, the fruit of paradise, the image of the whole round world with all its sensuality (see the plate on p.150). This group of Eve, the apple and the dragon is a silent and yet extremely eloquent protest against the old story of the Fall, a matriarchal anti-image. However, Eve is now no longer the primal mother of all life. She is a creation of God, but a creation resting in herself, successful and not fallen. And the dragon is no longer just the symbol of her fertility. Behind her stands Adam, not as successful as she, but the man to whom she belongs. The dragon with the apple in its mouth with which she is so lovingly associated is the world of wisdom, knowledge and sensual delight, to which she gives herself – of her own free will, in a sovereign way and without archaic compulsion.

Such images become increasingly rare in the modern period. However, the primal associations with women keep cropping up: woman and serpent, e.g. as an image of wisdom or level-headedness. Often these are only allegorical representations, but they contain the primal knowledge of the power and healing capacity of the woman, of the unity of mature human personality which can perhaps be depicted only in her, of wholeness.

At the Counter-Reformation an image became popular which in the form of a monument adorned many market places in Catholic South Germany and Italy and which was meant to demonstrate the final victory of the Christian patriarchal subjection of the world: the woman who tramples on the serpent's head. Really it is the mother church which – according to one translation of Gen.3.15 – is trampling on the serpent's head and with it on all that is alien, other, heretical. But at the same time this makes the woman herself the murderess of her senses and sexuality. In this image patriarchal images have even been developed to the point of absurdity. From now on 'pure' doctrine and the 'pure' woman belong together. The official process of purification had been successfully completed.

Yet the old tradition of women could not be exterminated. After the Thirty Years' War in Bad Teinach in the Black Forest a Protestant princess of Württemberg had an altar painted which is a non-patriarchal view of Christian salvation. Prompted by Jewish Kabbalah mysticism, she found the courage to have her own experiences of God expressed pictorially in the church of her spa, a woman's conception of salvation. Looked at closely, these pictures are a provocation to traditional conceptions of faith. On the outer wings of the didactic text ninety four female figures from the Bible are going to Christ – not a single man among them. Opening the wing discloses the princess herself as she contemplates salvation from her perspective. The scene is a garden with many plants which can be given an exact botanical identification. Biblical figures, patriarchs and prophets have their places in it. The whole is crowned with a cupola in which the Trinity, Father, Son and Spirit, can be seen in shadowy form in the background; but clearly, and in colour in the centre, there is a female Trinity: Father, Son and Holy Spirit are women. Kether is a copy of God the Father (reigning in the picture on the cupola above); Hokhmah, wisdom, in a red robe and blue coat, is at the same time the Son transported to God; Binah, depicted with tongues of fire, speaks the language of the Spirit, holds up the mirror of self-knowledge and, like the Cretan serpent goddess, has in her hand a serpent, the old symbol for the matriarchal unity of earth, life, salvation and woman (see the plate on p.104).[14]

It is not just the case that here a female person has been added to the male Trinity – a development that one can often find. Here there has been a matriarchal transformation of an experience of God which was tolerated and kept intact.

If we are to discover the history of women it is not enough to point to female elements in a religion which has been taken over by patriarchy. These elements often only provide all too painful evidence of the process of the transformation of a matriarchal into a patriarchal religion. Nor is it enough just to discover the counter-culture. Feminist research keeps coming up against a destroyed counter-culture of women, e.g. the witch culture. It seems to me that in addition there is a tendency to overlook the matriarchal sub-culture that has been preserved, reflecting women's own independent experience of freedom which was neither integrated and thus absorbed, nor destroyed, and which found expession in images and symbols – silently but eloquently.

Conceptions coming from a matriarchal context have kept alive in Christianity hidden basic human values and which were lost in the patriarchal pressure for conquest which are breaking out again today in dreams and imageries of a great many kinds:

woman's own worth,
the integration of nature, the body, the impulses,
the dream of a cosmic world of peace.

Part Three: A New Perspective on the Stories about Jesus and Women

Albrecht Dürer, 'Christ on the Mount of Olives'

8

THE WOMEN'S JESUS

Christ the Wholemaker

Ricarda Huch

Feminist christology?

From the beginning of the feminist movement the male redeemer Jesus has been a latent source of conflict for women frustrated by Christianity and one that has constantly been evaded. Moreover the maleness of Jesus has consequences – in the Catholic view – for the priesthood and the hierarchical structures of the church.

Mary Daly has spoken of 'Christolatry' in theology and expressed the expectation that 'a logical consequence of the liberation of women will be a loss of plausibility of christological formulas which reflect and encourage idolatry in relation to the person of Jesus'.[1] The story of Jesus, the person of Christ is the place where we ultimately decide whether a feminist religion is enough for us or whether a feminist Christian theology has something else to give us.

Rosemary Ruether has demonstrated how christology patriarchalized itself, how it became embedded in the church and its thought-patterns which were developing in a hierarchical way, how Christ the human being became Christ the man and the basic model for Christian life and church leadership.[2] Thus Jesus also became the contemporary ideal for man: a captain in the Zwinglian Reformation, a gentle but male superstar in modern times and a pioneer (Visser't Hooft) in our present lack of orientation.[3] He became what males were, wished, hoped to be. The honorific titles king, judge, prophet could even fade. As society became more democratic, Jesus too became more brotherly, more human. The brother Jesus, the brotherly Christ, was experienced existentially; he walked the streets with the lost – above all in the Christian lyricism of the Second World War. He became the new symbol for brotherhoods, the brotherly church, brotherly sharing. The brother was different from the lord and master: compassionate, sympathetic. But in that case he remained above all a brother of brothers, caught in their male spirit and in their thought world. The brotherhoods did not become sister groups. The suspicion arose among women that Big Brother had taken the place of the Great Father, who now spoke as representative of the sisters.

However, alongside the christology that developed along patriarchal lines at a very early stage there were alternative christologies which sought to stress forgotten female features: for example the androgynous christology of the mystics which sees Christ as the representative of a new humanity combining male and female elements.[4] Here, however, Christ represents the male as the normal human personality. Femininity is its lower bodily aspect. This christology seeks to reconcile what has been divided, but in the last resort remains androcentric. Or there is spiritual christology, above all that of the mediaeval Joachimites, who see Christ as the embodiment of the spirit of a new age which discloses itself in a female form in a second revelation or in individual persons. Both models keep cropping up in the history of the church and in cultural history among sub-cultures and sects down to the present. They are an important protest which shows how people would not be content with what had been thought out for them by the church and how their own experiences of faith and life could break open fossilized traditions. They are above all symbols of resistance, and they went under – perhaps also because women who at first had a place everywhere ultimately lost their influence.

The images which mothers before us had of Christ – as far

as we can glimpse them – are an example of the way in which our own pictures hand down the tradition: women have revered Christ as feminine wisdom, as the Nag Hammadi finds show.[5] Christ appeared to the Montanist Priscilla as a woman: 'Christ came to me in the form of a woman clothed in a radiant garment, implanted wisdom in me and revealed that this place is holy and that here Jerusalem will descend from heaven.'[6] Julian of Norwich spoke of Jesus the Mother: 'In Jesus, our true mother, has our life been grounded... and until the Day of Judgment he feeds and helps us on, just as we would expect the supreme and royal nature of motherhood to act.'[7] These examples – which also come from the sub-culture – can be continued at will, and they are still being discovered. New attempts are emerging from contemporary women's research: with the help of depth psychology the male Jesus has meanwhile become more human and also more attractive to women. Hanna Wolff depicted Jesus as the mature integrated human being who has integrated the male (*animus*) and the female (*anima*) and who was 'the first to break through the androcentrism of the ancient world'.[8] For Christa Mulack this integration of the *anima* was not, however, something that Jesus received in the crib. He had to undergo a laborious process of transformation. She describes this process in her interpretation of the story of the Canaanite woman:

> Only if the male recognizes itself and its own shadow, where it is prepared to renounce its pride and listen to the female, to serve it with its powers, by taking account of its needs and thus perceiving it in its complete humanity, can the female be healed; there the miracle of healing takes place, there it can be restored in its full human worth. And in this way the Son of Man learns what it means to bring people salvation.[9]

Jesus analysed in this way creates a model of human behaviour and makes it possible to see new aspects in the stories about Jesus and women. However, on the other hand this method runs the risk of forcing a contemporary cult of femininity on history, which contains more than psychological doctrines of salvation.

Feminist research into matriarchy sees in the image of the goddess who holds the dead hero in her bosom as an image of the dying and rising of nature, an image – which appears later as the Christian *pieta* – of the woman as the origin of life. However, the line which can be drawn from the hero, this vegetation hero, to the life and death of Jesus,[10] is thin and fragmentary; such interpretation passes over the story of Jesus and has it atrophied into a myth.

Women's research which is more strongly orientated on theology makes it possible to see Jesus again as Sophia (see above), to replace the old christology with a sophialogy which – as Felix Christ thinks – was one of the earliest christologies.[11] The wisdom which walks the streets and calls its children, the wisdom which is rejected by men, which was before creation and played in the presence of God, is a fascinating counterpart to the honorific titles and the brother-theologies.

However, the Jesus of the New Testament, the Jesus of the stories about women, can hardly be forced into becoming a principle, far less a female one. He evades this as he evades analysis, heroizing, and as he escapes glorification in male terms or being made into a brother. It seems to me that we best counter the idolatry of the person of Christ by enquiring again into his life in the context of human relationships. How did women find him?

By looking at the stories of women in the New Testament from an unconventional perspective and abandoning our inculcated tendency to develop -ologies, we can sharpen our senses and again learn to detect what happened between the women and Jesus: what we see, trace, feel today, what we did not see at an earlier stage, because we did not dare to begin the quest.

The activity of women

The stories about Jesus and women exercise an enormous dynamic once we forget that Jesus is the saviour, redeemer, Son of Man, Son of God or Messiah. We unleash this dynamic once we detach ourselves from what we have learned, what is above us, what is on our backs and smites our conscience. If we tone down our hierarchical thought-patterns, we detect that in many stories this dynamic comes from the women. So they are the active ones who set the process in motion and finally achieve something:

The woman with the issue of blood approaches from the midst of the crowd around Jesus, grasps his garment and is healed (Mark 5.25ff.).

The Canaanite woman cries after him until she is rebuked by the disciples. She has to make Jesus aware in a painful way that he is also there for her daughter (Matt.15.21ff.).

Martha plays a part in what some commentators find an impatient and loquacious way in the ultimate resurrection by Jesus of Lazarus. There is a direct relationship between her active nature and his passivity (John 11.19f.).

Jesus' mother is the first to note that the wine has run out at the wedding and asks her son to do something. The result is a dismissive rebuke, 'Woman, what have I to do with you' (John 2.1ff.).

We can meet similar observations from the theology of the handicapped today.

A woman pastor who made children with leukaemia paint Jesus saw in amazement that the children drew Jesus as the passive figure, with arms hanging down, whom the children had to stimulate and make active.

Three times we have accounts of women who entered strange houses brazenly and independently and anointed Jesus, i.e. performed symbolic actions which pointed to his death, his

121

burial and his role as messiah. The town prostitute anointed the feet of Jesus in the house of a Pharisee (Luke 7.36ff.); an unknown woman anointed his head at a meal in the house of Simon (Mark 14.3); and Mary, who was always restrained and shy, showed Jesus this physical kindness and becomes the centre of a scene which does not concern her (John 12.1ff.). On Easter morning these women then continued their activity – which seemed almost pointless – by visiting the grave of the enemy of the state in order to anoint his body (Mark 16.1ff.; Luke 24.1ff.).

So the women are in no way merely the women who go around after him, who 'serve' him in the bourgeois understanding of the term, who surround a great guru with friendship and listen to his words. The consequence of this activity among women is that Jesus changes. From being the nationalist who wants to limit himself to his own people, thanks to the Canaanite woman Jesus also becomes the helper and healer of the Gentiles, the Canaanites.

The man Jesus becomes impure, i.e. socially and culturally isolated, when the woman with an issue of blood touches him. He is quite taken by surprise and feels the strength leaving him (Mark 5.30f.).

The vacillator who sometimes seems passive and takes so much time before he raises Lazarus becomes the one who raises his dead friend as a result of the activity of a woman (John 11.19ff.).

In the Gospel of John, the miracle with the wine, initiated at the wedding by a woman, is the first introduction to his saving actions. The anointings by women, above all that by the unknown woman, point out his life and his way to him and make him aware of what he is for them, make him ready for what he is to be, prepare him for a dying that will be a defeat and yet will be accompanied by understanding and friendship.

The women get something from him: salvation, health, life, wine and humanity; and at the same time they give him something: meaning, tasks, a goal in life and that community without which our tasks and goals become remote from humanity and abstract. They get strength to live and invest in him hope, trust, visions which transcend him. They make him what he is by going with him on his way: the human being for all human beings, the solitary one who can be a comforting image for all who are solitary, the one who trusts in himself and can give self-confidence to all, a person who goes to death and yet is not alone.

Jesus grows through people, above all through and with women. He did not get anything in his cradle. He suffered by learning obedience (Heb.5.8). Still in Mark he is dependent in what he does on the atmosphere: 'He could not do a single thing there' (Mark 6.5), we are told of him in Nazareth. Even in Matthew this humanity has been retouched in favour of holiness. Jesus is already master of the situation: 'And he did not do many mighty works there' (Matt.13.58) runs the parallel passage. He is already on the way towards being a miracle worker, who bears within himself a divine mystery independently of human beings. And he is already on the way towards losing his humanity.

Again, Jesus draws strength from his encounters with women: he asks the Samaritan woman at the well to give him something to drink. He does not take from her what she is and has, her symbol of being water and vessel, even if he gives 'the water of life', and he finally makes her the apostle of the Samaritans (John 4.6ff.).

He draws energy from Martha's doggedness, from her love for her brother, for life. And in dialogue with him she became the one who makes a confession of Christ which is similar to that of Peter: 'You are the Christ, the Son of God, who has come into the world' (John 11.27).

Rembrandt has retained something of this attitude to Jesus in an impressive way in a pen-drawing of the healing of Peter's mother-in-law (see the plate on p.136). Jesus wants to raise the sick, feverish woman. He grasps her by the hands and power seems to go from him over to her, in such a way that both are involved in a relationship of force. Neither can let go of the other without falling. Both their forces are irredeemably bound together, even when the woman is raised from the floor and Jesus has ground under his feet. This dynamic, this play of forces, this exchange of energy, cannot be seen in other healings and encounters with males.

Our image of Jesus the supremely powerful miracle worker has disguised the fact that human beings draw this power from themselves. Our image, so abundant in the tradition, of the useless, sinful human being has made us forget how active people were. A dogmatic anxiety about Pelagianism (human beings having a share in salvation) prevents us from seeing healing processes going forth from human beings. The stories of Jesus with women show what is important for all healings: human activity, our own step towards becoming whole. However, that does not mean that we ourselves arrange our own salvation. But the power which we draw from ourselves, which becomes healing, is our own power.

And the power which people get from themselves turns into power which changes those who give energy; for the power, the confidence that we get for ourselves becomes confidence that we invest in others. This is a mutuality in which autonomy arises, in which autonomy develops, in which wholeness can be experienced: complete receptiveness and complete activity. No person has himself killed, gives himself up or sacrifices himself on the basis of a helper-syndrome.

This experience of mutuality coming from the stories of Jesus with women has many consequences. But so far they have hardly been noted.

The senses

We can also trace enormous sensuality in these encounters. Head, hands, feet are set in motion. Hair and clothes create warmness and intimacy. Things that destroy life, like fever and loss of blood, are stopped. Anointing brings coolness and savour; eating restores circulation and life. The word, which became so overpowering above all in the Protestant churches, is only accompaniment to this experience of the senses. The feverish, bleeding woman, the dead daughter of Jairus, they all *feel* something when they return to life. It is also said sometimes in connection with the healing of males that Jesus touched the sick. But many encounters with men run their course through conversations, questions and discussions. Their centre is elsewhere and their dynamic is restricted.

However, we sadly note that even within the New Testament a phobia over touching develops. The story of the woman with the issue of blood is no longer told in detail in Matthew. In Mark, the 'source of her bleeding dried up'. The woman felt in her whole body that she had been healed from her torment. And Jesus in turn immediately felt the power which had gone out from him (5.29f.). In Matthew this touching of the clothes of Jesus takes places only in the woman's thoughts (9.21). Nor does Jesus hold the hand of Peter's sick mother-in-law in Matthew; he only touches it in a symbolic way (cf. Mark 1.31; Matt 8.15). A process of spiritualization has set in to which much that is archaic and original falls victim: the miracles are toned down and shifted to words of Jesus. Dramatic scenes like the storm on the lake lose their vividness. The evil spirits are no longer described in so spooky a way. One almost feels that the Christians of the second generation were ashamed of their elemental, primal experiences.

But Mark is still earthy. He is the only one to tell the parable of the earth, the mother earth, which brings forth completely of its own accord (4.26f.) while human beings are sleeping. In him wind and storm are like people whom Jesus commands: 'Be silent and dumb!' And his Jesus, too, is earthy. He sleeps on a cushion in a boat (4.38); he is sorrowful, sighs, is angry (Mark 8.12; 3.5; 10.14). He loves the rich young man with agape, the mutual love which does not come from above (Mark 10.21; but cf. Matt.19.21). He embraces the children and does not use them for a lesson (Mark 10.16; 9.36; cf. Matt.19.15;

18.2). The later accounts have blotted out the anger (cf. Matt.12.9f.; Mark 3.5) and produced the emotionless Son of God, in whom there is also less room for grief and for tenderness (cf. Mark 1.41 with Matt.8.3; Mark 10.16 with Matt.9.15). It can even be said of the original Jesus that he had an 'unclean spirit' (Mark 3.30) and that his family thought that he was 'mad' (Mark 3.21). In his dismay over his own career this Markan Jesus falls to the earth in Gethsemane (14.35), the earth which later receives him, the earth over which there was darkness for three hours before his death, the earth which in the parable told by Mark brings forth of its own accord. The earth accepts sorrow, suffers, gives up – in Matthew – its dead, just as in the old matriarchal myth Demeter makes the earth mourn and go on strike until her daughter Persephone, of whom she has been robbed by the god of the underworld, returns again. No heavenly resolution has yet transcended this earthiness. In Mark Jesus is already overwhelmed [the German phrase used for this is literally 'goes to ground', producing a word-play which is impossible to render in English] in Gethsemane, and not on the cross. This scene in Mark is hardly noticed and almost never depicted in art. The one who is raised up to the Father, the Son who suffers at his hands and is obedient to the end, the man of grief on the cross, who hangs on the symbol of redemption – these are the typical leading images. However, at least two portrayals have retained the suffering which forces one to the ground, the kind that is normally experienced by men:

On a narrow picture in the margin of Codex Rossanensis from the sixth century Christ is crouched down, huddled on the ground in anxiety, his face turned downwards – an attitude which recalls many representations of the great 'sinner' Mary Magdalene bent over Jesus' feet. Moon and stars can be seen against a dark blue background. Jesus is delivered over to the night without any relief.[12]

A pen drawing by Dürer from 1521 depicts the Mount of Olives not as an 'elevation' – as so often – but as a landscape with terraces on which Christ lies with arms stretched out in the form of a cross, abandoned, without hope, earthly, fixed to the ground, and yet embracing the earth, without falling into the abyss (see plate p. 116).

But in the main theological tradition Jesus had long passed over to the side of the light, as the one who overcomes. The dark side of his human existence, without which his heavenly figure is inconceivable, was suppressed. In Carolingian art, which took over the old triumphal symbolism, he clearly stands on the right side, the side of the sun. However, an ivory relief from the year 1000 shows the crucifixion scene for once reversed: as usual sun and moon are put on the right- and left-hand side respectively. But here the moon is depicted as the face of Christ with the nimbus of the cross. It thus has a higher significance than the sun: here the night side is regarded as the basic experience of human existence, and at the same time it is the image of repressed female reality. It is an exception in iconography, but it is an example of a possible alternative interpretation of the story of Jesus.[13]

People can have communion with this Jesus with a heart, with anger, who suffers, heals, surrenders himself, and goes under. An emotionless Son of God from whom anger has been obliterated and whose warmth is reduced in favour of obedience could only give and expect discipleship, and no longer have any two-way relationship.

According to Anton Mayer, the decisive and fatal shift within New Testament religion between Jesus and Paul is 'a shift in the experience of the senses': 'specifically in the shift from eye to ear and thus from freedom to obedience'.[14]

Parallelism

The third thing to be noted in the story of Jesus with women is that sayings about the women and about Jesus run parallel, but that these can clearly be seen only in Mark. As I have already pointed out, Elisabeth Schüssler-Fiorenza has observed that *diakonein* – serve – is used of both the women and of Jesus. In terms of social history this serving describes the situation of those whose situation is utterly inferior and who have to do the worst work. For service is often understood as serving tables and 'at meals in antiquity there were very strict hierarchical rules according to which the servant was the one who was lowest in the social scale, either the slave or the son or the daughter or the wife'.[15]

It is said of the women that they had followed Jesus, served him and gone up with him to Jerusalem (Mark 15.41). When she is healed, Peter's mother-in-law also serves (Mark 1.31). What is said of the women is now also said of Jesus: 'The Son of man did not come to be served but to serve, and to give his life as a ransom for many' (Mark 10.45). Serving is the characteristic behaviour in the new community; it is the renunciation of rule and hierarchical order: it shows 'the eschatological reversal of all power-relationships among men' (Luise Schottroff). 'You know,' runs a saying of Jesus, 'that those who are supposed to rule over the Gentiles lord it over them, and their great men exercise authority over them. But it shall not be so among you; but whoever would be great among you must be your servant' (Mark 10.42ff.). Whereas the disciples still expect to hold places of honour in the kingdom of God, women already represent something of this new order.

In Mark, something is said interchangeably of the women and Jesus which brings them into a unique mutual relationshp. Discipleship – *akolouthein* – accepting the possibility of execution, i.e. living without compromise and with readiness for risk, is used of many of them. Moreover some of them risked going up to Jerusalem and thus sharing in the way of the passion, and they were later regarded as witnesses of the crucifixion. However, serving, accepting a non-hierarchical order throughout one's existence, seems to have been a specific characteristic of the women and Jesus.[16] A 'non-hierarchical vision of human connection' (Carol Gilligan) is noted today in women's psychology.[17] Accordingly the women would have had an essential, formative share in Jesus' life-style and view of life. At least they would have made possible an atmosphere in which such a concept could be maintained.

In order to understand the scope of this Marcan comment rightly, we must at the same time become aware of the deletions which Matthew and Luke made in it:

Neither Matthew nor Luke have maintained this three-dimensionality of uncompromising, alternative and authentic life of the kind embodied by the women in Mark (15.41). At this point Matthew still combines discipleship and service (Matt.27.55). Luke has only retained discipleship (Luke 23.49), and in his Gospel serving is already on the way to becoming a function which is exclusive to women. The women serve Jesus and the disciples, who have already become an élite celibate group. The Lucan church is the church on the way to our traditional distribution of roles.

There is a further parallel between the women and Jesus: the same strong expression, 'being shattered', 'being shaken to the core and terrified' (*ekthambeisthai*) is used – again only in Mark – of Jesus in Gethsemane and of the women at the empty tomb (Mark 14.33; 16.5). It is only used once elsewhere, of the people when they see Jesus again after his transfiguration (Mark 9.15). The weaker word *thambeisthai* is used of the disciples (Mark 10.24,32) and the people (Mark 1.27), similarly in situations where they receive a shock.

It seems to me significant that two different situations which both times confront people with an abyss in their previous experience, the empty tomb and Gethsemane, are associated by the same emotive word. There is something of the same quality about the experience of grief, shock and anxiety for both Jesus and the women. The later Gospels no longer risked expressing the same degree of emotion between the Son of God and human beings. In Matthew the gentler 'be sorrowful' has taken the place of the 'being shaken to the core' (26.37). In Luke Jesus is the one who prays vigorously and no longer the one who is desperate and disturbed.

Another close connection between women and Jesus can be seen in the scenes of crucifixion, death and burial. The way in which the women look on in Mark and Matthew is denoted with the word *theorein* (Matt.27.55: 28.1; Mark 15.40,47; 16.4). That is more than simply watching. It is perceiving, understanding, knowing, a total comprehension which is identical with the 'knowing the signs which Jesus did' in John (2.23; 7.3). The onlookers take in the one on whom they look and identify with him. This is a communicative knowledge. The women are 'true theoreticians' of what happened at Golgotha.

This understanding and grasping is not the intellectual, conceptual ordering, understanding, having. It is being caught up in the event, affected, wounded. In their separation from the one whom they continue to observe from a distance – in contrast to the disciples, who have fled – they experience his death. In their forsakenness they experience his God-forsakenness. His burial which they observe has nothing intrinsically final in itself, but bears the germ of hope for them. He has been removed from the brutal violence of human control. They can restore something of the lost relationship: the oil with which they seek to anoint the body on Easter morning is a symbol of something of the old relationship and a piece of new hope. But since they have not abandoned him in death they finally experience that God has not abandoned him (see the plate on p.62). Since they are the only ones to go to his grave, they hear the message of resurrection. Had they not gone with him, there would be no Easter message. Without the mutual community, experienced and maintained, we would not have experienced any hope of resurrection.

In Luke the total comprehension of the death of Jesus as expressed in the term *theorein* has been abandoned. The women simply 'look' (*theasthai, horan*). They are onlookers, but not complete theoreticians, theologians.

In an investigation of 'suffering' made on the basis of accounts by handicapped people, Erika Schuchardt came to ask why theology has so little to say in this respect, why it does not understand suffering in a much more specific way as being abandoned and does not reflect on the intertwining of God's preservation and human companionship which is experienced by the handicapped person.

'Can one develop a "theology of suffering" without bringing in these two dimensions of relationship as the decisive experience? Is God's gift to human beings, the capacity for relationship, sufficiently taken account of in theology?

Is there reflection in theology as to what ambivalent forces are constantly at work to cripple this capacity?

Would it not be the task of theology as a partner of other disciplines again to prompt discussion of the dimension beyond our control of a capacity for relationships without anxiety over losing its academic character?'[18]

The background to these parallel statements about Jesus and the women, God and humanity, is Mark's mysticism. 'All things are possible with God' (Mark 10.27). 'All things are possible to him who believes' (Mark 9.23). Only he makes this bold identification between God and the believer. The later Gospels no longer dare to venture this parallelism between God and human possibility. Human possibilities now have support. Of course all remains possible with God. But this statement is immediately connected with another one to balance it: 'With men this is impossible' (Matt.19.26). The story of the rich young man is an example of this. Even Mark tells it as a story of failure, but not in the establishment of mutual love. But alongside this, for him there is also the awareness of the knowledge of the mutuality of the power of God and man.

In iconography such conceptions have later found expression above all in the Martha tradition. More than any other woman she is set alongside Jesus, is made to conform to him: in Gethsemane in a picture by Fra Angelico,[19] at the resurrection in raising the dead and healing the sick, in the paintings of the baroque church dedicated to Martha in Porlezza (Italy), and in the Martha altar at Nuremberg, where she solemnly invites Jesus into her house. The miracle-worker's staff which Jesus uses in early Christian representations for raising Lazarus passes over to her and later in her hand becomes the cross-staff with which she binds the dragon.[20] These unusual portrayals are to be found, however, predominantly in mediaeval sub-culture; they disappeared almost completely at the beginning of modern times.

A bold parallelism between the experience of Jesus and that of women seems to me still to be present in the helpless endurance of brutality depicted in the numerous mediaeval figures of the crucified woman. According to the legend she is said to have been married by her father to a pagan husband whom she did not love. Instead of this she betrothed herself to Christ and asked him to deform her by giving her a beard; thereupon her royal father had her crucified. The figure with a beard and long garment which appears above all in the eastern Alps is called, among other things, *liberatrix* = female liberator, and is even now treated as a legendary, painful artistic mistake – like some similar modern pictures!

Seen from the perspective of women, Jesus displays a side of his humanity which is hardly seen in christology: his capacity for relationship, the need to enter into creative dialogue with people, and also the tragedy of failing them. Here it becomes evident that he already practised with others – above all with women – a non-hierarchical ordering of society based on mutuality.

At the same time it is also evident that this mutual life-style was already overpainted during the writing of the Gospels with conceptions of the exalted Son of God, who no longer needed human relationships.

Excursus: The imperial Christ

The degree to which the understanding of Christ in Christianity developed contrary to the traditions of women and became adapted to the model of lordship is evident from the descriptions of Christ in the first millennium. In particular the representation of the *Christus victor* was adapted to the triumphal imperial iconography in which the victor put his foot on the neck of the conquered. This *calcatio*, treading with the foot, was one of the main ceremonies with which the victor celebrated his triumph.

In the fourth century the political *calcatio* was almost inseparable from the image of the rule of Christ. In the age of Constantine Christ takes the place of the victorious Caesar, whose emblems now become Christian symbols. Claims to lordship characteristic of the ancient Near East passed over into Christianity through the claims of the Roman emperor. We already find echoes of the *calcatio* in the Old Testament: Ps.91.13; Gen.3.15; Isa.11.8. It also appears in the New Testament at I Cor.15.25.

Christ becomes the victor over the dragon, the serpent, the lion – in patriarchal understanding evil, demonic powers, which were nevertheless really the feminine symbols for life, salvation and renewal. He treads on them so that they have no more claims. Even the labarum, the cross-staff, can be used as a means of this. Only in thirteenth-century art do these symbols lose significance.

However, from the eighth century on the spear-thrust into the dragon's mouth also becomes typical of Western typology. It is taken over in representations of Michael which in turn go back to classical patriarchal representations of victory over the dragon (Heracles). Now the victory over opponents ends pictorially with the death, the final elimination, of the opponent, the old world.

Still, there are some deviations from these militant pictures of Christ. On a book cover in the Bodleian Library from the ninth century Christ is also standing on the serpent, but it is coiling itself by his side towards his hand, which contains a book with the inscription 'Jesus Christ over the aspis'. On the cover of the Lorch Evangeliar from about 810 there is a free serpent beside the conquered serpent, moving alongside Christ. The symbol of matriarchal 'wisdom' and sagacity has a relationship to Christ and is not just done away with, annihilated.[21]

Deviations from Christian militancy can also be seen on the Scottish cross of Ruthwell from the eighth century. Here too Christ is standing above the animals, but these have raised and crossed their forepaws and are worshipping Christ as saviour of the world: integration instead of annihilation.[22] This representation, which seems to come from Iro-Scottish conceptions with a matriarchal stamp, is closer to the Gospels and their view of the cosmic incorporation of the powers (e.g. Mark 1.13). In the Gospels the powers 'obey': wind, sea, demons obey Jesus, but not human beings (Matt.8.25 par.; Mark 1.27). Old Testament images of Leviathan who comes from God's sphere of power (Job 40;41) also match this representation. A Christ throned directly on the animals and sitting on a dragon throne similarly depicts Christ as the Lord of the animals, but not as their annihilator.[23]

However, these two representations are rare. The christology of the West associated with the representations of Christ as lord do not seek cosmic breadth, but victory and annihilation of the alien. The Western Christ became the restrictive Lord who made one culture characterized by lordship and domination. Whereas the Eastern church understood the resurrection as the descent into hell and the ascent from it again, and made this its pictorial type, in the West the victorious Christ won the day. The human, saving images of Christ who with large hands seizes the over-large hands of the dead and raises them up, was better able to reproduce the unity of darkness and light, of death and resurrection, than the annihilator of the dragon in the militant West.

Christ healing Peter's mother-in-law. Rembrandt, about 1659

MUTUALITY

> Finally someone who has deliberately undergone his own
> destiny in all its tragedy will also detect more clearly and more
> rapidly the suffering of the other, even if he must go beyond it.
> He will not be able to mock strange feelings of any kind if he
> can take his own seriously. He will no longer go round the
> vicious circle of contempt.
>
> *Alice Miller*

Women discover mutuality

Feminist theology in the USA has sometimes already understood itself as a theology of mutuality. Mutuality seems to
be becoming a keyword of feminist theology, even if it is
approached in different ways. As far as I can see, Isabel Carter
Heyward was the first to set out a theology of mutuality in a
published dissertation, *The Redemption of God. A Theology
of Mutual Relation*.[1] She, too, sees the Gospel of Mark as an
unexploited source for as yet undeveloped perspectives from
the gospel relating to the capacity of contemporary people for
mutuality. For her Jesus was not unique. But his relationship
to God was unique, a unique liberating relationship which
anyone can have with God.

Following her, in 1981 Beverly Wildung Harrison stressed
the lack of relationship in traditional Christian theology. She
recalls how 'I still think with horror how often during the years
when I was studying theology I was warned by someone who
wrote a good deal about Christian ethics not to confuse true
Christian love with mere mutuality... Mutual love is... love in
its deepest radical nature. If we are to experience it we must

be open, we must be in a position to give and receive. It is tragic that a reified male Christianity cannot teach us to be such lovers.'[2] Here it is clear that there is a late-capitalist tendency constantly to speak of 'relationships' and 'capacity for relationships'. However, in feminist experience relationships are not packed and sold as goods; here women begin from the recognition of the deep total sociality of all things: 'Everything is bound up together'. Hence 'relationship' also takes on a cosmological and critical ecological significance. However, lack of relationship must inevitably grow out of a theological tradition which imagines God as being autonomous and unrelated, because this experience of transcendence teaches only the possible free resolution for relationships.

Rosemary Ruether similarly speaks of a theology of mutual relationships and already sees that the relationship between the redeeming Christ and redeemed women is to be understood in dynamic terms. The redeemer, too, is one who has been redeemed, as Jesus accepted the baptism of John.[3] However, Ruether has not attached any specific role to the activity and the activating dynamism of women.

To me the New Testament with its stories about Jesus seems to be a still undisclosed source for 'mutuality', its successes and failures. Alongside the stories of Jesus and women the stories about Jesus and the disciples need to be looked at here. Only the two together provide a source from which we can understand the early Christian conceptions of mutuality and make them come alive in the present.

First of all, contemporary ideas from psychotherapy help us to understand better the situation of the women around Jesus and the disciples.

Positive and negative mutuality

In psychotherapy today there is talk of 'positive' and 'negative mutuality'.[4] In some respects this corresponds to the relationship of the women to Jesus and the relationship of the disciples to him.

Positive mutuality is characterized by a movement of relationship. Its character is dialogue, but is in no way limited to speaking. Complex psychological spheres and processes are involved here. Feelings which give colour and vehemence, pleasure and disgust to actions and reactions, are an essential element. The movement is also a movement of mutual recognition and therefore goes more deeply into the mutual satisfaction of need. It links up with what Hegel has called the duplication process of self-awareness; if we relate to the other as the object of our needs, our initiatives, our orientation on the world, this other must always also be a subject for us, remain the centre of his or her own needs, his or her own initiative and orientation. Only in this way does he or she remain autonomous, someone over against us. The third essential characteristic is confrontation with the partner. Room must be kept for opposition and conflict. Without them there can be no authentic mutuality.

We were able to observe the first two characteristics of positive mutuality in the relationship between the women and Jesus: the dialogue of feelings, actions, remaining a person, recognizing the autonomy of the other, the person in encounter. The third characteristic, confrontation, seems to me to be contained in the resurrection narratives. After the flight narrated in the first conclusion of Mark in which the women seek to avoid encounter with a wholly other Jesus, there is an encounter: in Matthew with a group of them, and in Mark and John with Mary Magdalene. The saying of Jesus to Mary Magdalene, 'Do not touch me', confronts her with a conflict which hitherto she had not perceived: Jesus is no longer the same, no longer at her disposal. She must go her way without him. This confrontation is also contained in the other resurrection stories. The old relationship has been interrupted. The women are given a task but no longer the ongoing nearness they desire.

An example of negative mutuality seems to me to be the relationship between the disciples and Jesus, above all as it is still contained in Mark.

Again, three characteristics are important for negative community. First, the disruption of the dialogical movement in affectivity, feelings and actions. Mark above all still clearly shows how from his brotherly fellowship of which Jesus says, 'He who does the will of God is my brother and my sister and my mother' (Mark 3.35), a group comes into being whose 'heart is hardened' (Mark 6.52; 8.17), a group which does not understand, which does not develop mutual feelings and sensibility. The critical scene there is depicted in a very vivid way: the disciples have returned, tired from preaching and healing, and Jesus invites them to rest awhile and goes with them in a ship to a lonely place. He knows about their exhaustion and takes account of their physical condition. The critical situation comes in the evening. Five thousand people have followed them; the disciples, exhausted and hungry, want to sent the people away and have the supper which they have brought with them: five loaves and two fishes. However, for Jesus it is impossible for them to segregate themselves in this way. He wants what they have brought with them to be shared. And in the end all are filled. But the disciples do not grow as a result of this experience: when Jesus comes towards them on the lake they have understood nothing of his cosmic power: 'They had not understood about the loaves and their hearts were hardened' (Mark 6.52). This reproach is repeated and further intensified: 'Are your hearts hardened? Having eyes do you not see, and having ears do you not hear? And do you not remember? I broke five loaves among five thousand people...'(8.18). They turn to stone, do not perceive, cannot take in what they have experienced. Their experiences take on no life. Jesus remains alone, in his activity and his feelings.

Matthew is already different. He tells the same stories, but without these emotional overtones and developments. There is no Jesus who accedes to the weary disciples. There is no mention of their stubbornness and lack of sensitivity, the hardened heart, beginning to turn to stone. For Matthew, Jesus' walking on the water, by which Mark shows the hardness of their hearts, is not an exemplary story. His problem is the lack of faith in the sinking Peter, who wants to imitate Jesus. In Matthew, Jesus' great outburst of disappointment, in which once again all the hardened senses of the disciples are addressed, is transformed into a didactic discourse which ends with the disciples understanding him (Matt.6.12). For him mutuality, whether positive or negative, was not a theme.

Disruption to the development of autonomy

The second characteristic of a disruption of mutuality is that the relationship becomes one-sided. No mutually confirmed autonomy develops between Jesus and the disciples in the course of their time together.

However, according to Mark this autonomy, mutuality, community did once exist. Following the call of the apostles he says: 'They (the disciples) went out and preached that men should repent. And they cast out many demons, and anointed with oil many that were sick and healed them' (Mark 6.12f.). The disciples also had independent discussions in Jesus' presence with the people and the scribes (9.14). John self-consciously asked Jesus about the credentials of someone 'who does not follow us' (9.38). From these traces of an autonomy in mutuality we can also see the traces of a mutuality which develops in a negative way: the disciples experience Jesus as overpowering. Here justice is not done to Jesus; he cannot be confirmed by the opposite side and the disciples in turn must turn away from one who is felt to be overpowering – in disappointment. When the way of the passion begins, two disciples, James and John, ask him for places of honour in glory (Mark 10.35ff.). They totally fail to understand the way of Jesus, and want to fulfil in him their needs for honour, well-being, reward for discipleship. They seek to regenerate themselves by means of their 'object' Jesus, but do not see his way, his task, his person, and cannot mature in relationship with him. Jesus is experienced as distanced from them; he becomes the Lord. They become servants. They can later compensate for this failure in mutuality through false strength, but the basic feeling of a lack of experience of mutuality remains normative and becomes a basis for many wrong modes of life and behaviour.

However, even Matthew and Luke already no longer wanted to note signs of such independence and personal activity. In the parallel text Matthew speaks in general terms of the power which will be given to the disciples over unclean spirits and for healing the sick (10.5ff.). He no longer mentions the fact that they have done this. Luke certainly mentions it, but it has already been summarized so that it becomes a pale comment: 'And they departed and went through the villages, preaching the gospel and healing everywhere' (9.6). Instead of the disciples, Jesus is already constantly the centre of discussion. In Matthew and Luke the scene which Mark has beginning with a discussion between the disciples, the people and the scribes (9.14) already brings the disciples and Jesus together again (Matt.17.14; Luke 9.37). The dynamics of encounter and movement, the fact that Jesus clashes with them, that they are a group and represent something in themselves, is no longer of interest. And Luke has changed the confused saying about 'following us', which does not occur in Matthew at all. In Luke, the sentence in Mark which read 'We (the disciples) saw a man casting out demons in your name who does not follow us and we forbade him, because he was not following us' (9.38) has become 'We saw a man casting out devils in your name, and we forbade him, because he does not follow you with us' (9.49). Luke can no longer can change the subsequent comment, which is probably an original saying of Jesus, 'He who is not against us is for us', at the expense of the disciples and in favour of an exalted Jesus. It shows how parallel to his disciples Jesus saw himself, how he identified himself with them, gave them value and status, instead of making himself one who walks alone.

The third characteristic of negative relationship is a failure for confrontation to take place. The disciples avoided it through flight. Judas avoided it through treachery and suicide. In the Easter encounters perhaps there is a repetition of the encounter that did not take place. The rent is stitched together. But the patched-up relationship, the shattered mutuality, needed an immense theological apparatus to become tenable. And it needed a hierarchical church. The reason why we can only perceive these conflicts from the perspective of women is that in Mark we still come up against remnants of such disrupted relationships. The other Gospels, like many theologies, have kept no mutuality and retouched the parallel passages relating to mutuality and growing alienation. In Matthew it is already the mothers and not the disciples themselves who ask for places of honour for their sons. Now there is less mention of experiences of the senses, of feelings, reactions of disciples and anxieties and outbursts of Jesus. Now the distance is cemented between the Son of God and children of God, which then justifies the distance of Christians from one another and their models of rule.

Male theology

Theology normally begins with the tradition of the fathers, disciples and brothers and repeats their experiences and feelings of guilt:

The disciples left Jesus and with him the power-play of mutual relationships. They left him and at the same time God left them. Their guilt has these two dimensions: their flight and his abandonment by God. Paul's experience is also the same. The beginning of his theological career is marked by guilt: the persecution of the community and thus guilt at Jesus. Thus the abyss of separation from God comes at the beginning

of male theology: 'Depart from me, for I am a sinful man...'
'I am he, I should repent...'

This theological reflection has silenced the distinctive experiences of women. It has brought us general sinfulness and detachment from Jesus. Who Jesus is is discussed in the hierarchical categories of priest, prophet and king. And if he was again brought near to men in mystical or Reformation outbursts and became contemporary and identical in form to them, then it was above all the griefs, lonelinesses, forsakennesses which people might share with him, not the interplay of forces. In Luther's 'joyful exchange' people exchange their misery for salvation. Here there is no question of the mutual play of forces. If people are to take their stand under the cross then these are not companionable, compassionate friends, but sinners full of guilt, self-hatred and contempt:

Me guilty, me refuse not,
Incline thy face to me.

There is no place in the mainstream theological culture in which the lostness of humanity is reflected for the Martha of the mediaeval sub-culture who watches with Jesus in Gethsemane, stands under the cross and supports the weak sisters.[5] The companionship which did not come about, the loss of mutuality, is compensated for. The failure resulted in strong words about the fight for faith and chivalry. Jesus became necessary as Lord and master. 'I needed a Lord!' Those who had to be strong and wanted to be strong needed a strong man and made him the victor, ruler, conqueror, hero who supported them in the battle against weakness, the flesh, the body and against all that was weak, seductive and markedly pleasurable.

The problems of male socialization extend into the Gospel. Individuation, self-assertion, the Father-Son conflict became theological thought-patterns. The inculcated pressure towards self-assertion became a conflict, and wanting to be like God the cardinal sin.

In that case the only appropriate domination was the domination of God. Mutuality was a piece of disorder which had a revolutionary potential. As Karl Barth wrote in 1934 to Henriette Visser't Hooft, 'There is no kind of mutual interest between God and humanity, only superiority!... You do not see clearly enough that there (I Cor.11) Paul's view of the superiority of the man is only a means to an end, in order to speak of the superiority of God over human being. Read the text again completely from this perspective, which of course should exclude any mutualism!'[6]

In certain phases of life, in some social experiences and forms of work, women have been able to find an identity without great difficutly. However, the more they become aware of themselves now, the more questionable they find the male socialization in faith which is forced on them. Their thought-patterns and models of life do not occur.

There is a legitimate, authentic male experience which is perceived in its forced and rational self-assertion, and there is a legitimate authentic male theology which reflects these conflicts and possible solutions. The difficult thing is when one-side male experience comes forward with the claim to be the experience of everyone. Too often male theology has claimed to be human theology.

Can the experience of women under the cross and by the tomb be introduced again? Can Christianity put feminine thought patterns and models in the place of male ones and alongside them?

Dynamic relationship

One important point which does not seem to me so far to have been noted is that a positive human mutuality encounters us from the stories about Jesus and women in the New Testament, which has consequences for theology and ethics. There is a mutuality which I have discovered from the women which is not just any old exchange of feelings, opinions, everyday experiences and so on. It is activated by an experience of deficiency which to begin with is an experience of social lack as a result of not being noticed, of emptiness, sickness, loneliness, defamation. In theological terminology we could also call it the experience and knowledge of 'sin'. This being empty is overcome actively in encounter with Jesus, in that women at the same time become open for encounter, become capable of accepting, receiving, healing. It is active receptiveness or, better, receptive activity. And a new social relationship arises out of it. A reality comes into being in that the one by whom a relationship, healing, is sought becomes a personality and takes on another form. The converse also happens in that the one whose powers are aroused in this encounter again discloses a free area in which personality can develop. These energies become permeable and mutually create new spheres of life.

In such a relationship there is always a source of power, which can also be seen objectively, a personality with emanation, strength, eroticism: Jesus, father, mother, teacher, and even a child or a sick person can be imagined. For example, in his radical humanity Jesus remains the pole of energies from which our energies come and from which we get our energies. The only important issue in our context is who triggers off the power and that these are of the kind that have never experienced an 'I'.

We know the hierarchical relationships, the social orders which also stamp personal relationships. The power goes, or at least seems to go, from above. The one below is a passive recipient. The one who is above thinks that he has to attach himself to the power, and any withdrawal is a personal threat. Below, this conduct is matched by obedience and distance. Contact is avoided as far as possible.

We also know the democratic, brotherly orders in which parity prevails. They are shaped by activity which deliberately aims at a gift in return: *do ut des*. Many of our relationships function within this structure. Our present social economy is governed by it. Many marriages, relationships between parents and children and friendships are built on giving and giving in return. However, that means that the breaks in these relationships are also programmed in advance. Parents who want to be rewarded by their child for their 'sacrifice' experience 'ingratitude' and become bitter. The secret hierarchical trend has yet to be overcome. The economy of *do ut des* begins from those who are actively strong and giving; the disappointment is that giving makes up the basic structure of human relationships. Moreover, the dependence of the one who receives is overlooked; he or she can only compensate for his or her passivity by giving, and continuing the circle of the strong. The end is general disillusionment about all that goes to make up human relationships.

I would term the relationship which comes from mutuality the energetic relationship which takes and gives, which takes by giving. It sets free forces which can develop in the hierarchial and brotherly order into domination, into male arrogance or female arrogance. In the energetic relationship receptivity is again taken seriously as a basis of human experience. It is fundamentally the experience of the child who looks to its mother and seeks food because of loneliness, hunger and the need for warmth. At the same time there is a glimpse of the power of those in our social order who or seen as 'weak' and 'only' receptive, in its explosive and changing side: just as the mother gets warmth and respect from her empty, hungry child, so those who seem weak, by supplying their needs, give others a strength of their own and a different value from that which comes from generous giving.

The basic pattern of this relationship is the relationship between mother and child. But at the same time it is deeply rooted in the exerience of women. The progress of women in their capacity for suffering and emotion which has been analysed and interpreted positively by Horst Eberhard Richter can become the activating and changing power.[7]

In this capacity for relationship our autonomy develops. This is no longer the Enlightenment autonomy and its rational, solitary, self-assertive I. It is an autonomy which feeds on basic emotional experiences and which nevertheless is not dissolved in a community that enables individuality and has a dynamic effect on community. It could be a model for partnership, friendship, conversation groups and not least for relationships between parents and children. It is contained in the early stories about women in the New Testament with their earthiness and sensuality, and it can awaken two things:

1. love for ourselves on the basis of our senses and earthly experiences:

2. love which is energetic, not hierarchical and no longer just brotherly and democratic, love which could change all our attitudes.

Eve, Rheims cathedral, about 1400

10

SELF-LOVE

I am a woman
I am a Filipino
I live
I fight
I hope

I am made in God's image
like all people in the world
I am a human being with value and worth
I think
I feel
I act

I am the little I am
before the great I AM.

Elizabeth Tapie

Justification and acceptance

Anyone who lives by the power of the God who loves unconditionally is accepted with all his or her existence, from top to
toe, inside and out, negative and positive. Anyone who lives
in this sphere of God's life must today be able to say:'I am
good. I am whole. I am beautiful.'

I came to this principle from two sides: first, from the
experience of the depth of self-hatred in women and the slight
degree to which the liberating message of the gospel can
change anything here; and second, from reflecting on the
centre of Protestant theology, the awareness of the liberation

of human beings without their own effort, of their unconditional acceptance.

In technical theological language this centre of Protestant theology is called the doctrine of justification. This expression seems to be comprehensible only to a limited professional world or to an older generation. The abstract legalistic expression sends cold shivers down the spines of many women. For me personally it was always a key to the social breadth and possibility of personal development in Christianity, so let us reflect briefly on its origin and significance.

The basic narrative of the unconditional acceptance of human beings – as they are, in whatever state, self-confident, ruined, alienated, happy, sick – is the New Testament parable of the prodigal son. This story is the centre of Christian theology and for all ages, churches and societies contains revolutionary tinder, since the experience that God unconditionally accepts searching, immoral, doubting human beings initially undermines any expectation of good social behaviour. In the course of church history this basic experience has been given different interpretations depending on individuals or their culture. For Paul, freedom from the law, from the Jewish law, was the basic experience rooted in Christ which led him to discover that the gospel is also for the Gentiles, for those who are remote from God. For Luther the duties which the church expected to be performed in a life in accordance with God caused a conflict which led to the proclamation of the freedom from such works, the freedom of a Christian. The prodigal sons are those who come to grief on the meaninglessness of their own achievements, who forget their own achievements and return to their Father with nothing but trust. According to Erich Fromm, this doctrine of Luther's thus contains a hidden matriarchal element – despite its 'manifest patriarchal character'.[1] For one cannot earn a mother's love. One either has it or one does not. All that one can do is to turn oneself into a helpless, powerless child and to have trust.

In the Lutheran theology which developed later, however,

this approach was changed into a legalistic theory of satisfaction according to which the sacrificial death of Christ is the foundation for the legal act of our acceptance by God. The elements of spontaneity and affectivity which Luther still used to describe this experience of God (*sua sponte*) were thus choked by the conception of a Father God who judges and calls for satisfaction.

As a result of psychoanalysis and above all through Paul Tillich, who was strongly influenced by depth psychology, the old doctrine of justification was revived in the concept of acceptance.[2] People need to be accepted and affirmed if they are to live. Without this experience they die. Accepting oneself therefore also means integrating those parts of the personality which have so far been suppressed and denied, the inferior parts, one's own shadow. The prodigal sons are those who can accept themselves in the knowledge of the destructive and unperceived dimensions in themselves and in God.

This form of the old doctrine of justification has again taken on new life in therapeutic pastoral care. In conversation there is experience of personal companionship and personal experience through the old form of the appropriation of the kerygma of acceptance by God. The historically-conditioned legalistic element fades. The primal history again comes to the fore: regaining one's own worth, being restored to the status of child, of son – the experience of God which does not destroy the human self.[3]

But what can this mean for women today?

They are not sons, they are not Gentiles, they are not tormented by what the church requires. And they have already heard enough preaching about self-acceptance. This has perhaps made them more relaxed, more sensitive to psychological developments, but the basic discrepancy which has arisen today between a negative self-image which is experienced in society and church and the gospel of the equal rights of men and women has not been affected by this. Acceptance can only be communicated credibly in a credible sphere or through an authentic personality. It needs more than words: atmosphere, social framework, personal integrity.

In periods of social revolution the gospel of the revolution of all personal values and its message of the liberating power of God in the individual has always had a revolutionary potential. Can that also be said for women who are being liberated today? It seems to me to be important to recall some elements of this experience of liberation, to see whether they have anything to offer women in extending their contemporary experiences.

I am good

This is a Reformation principle which unfortunately has been suppressed among us. In Christian experience and theological culture, being good no longer has a proper place. We are more familiar with the experience of being 'bad', and of the theological language of being a sinner. We are aware of our mistakes; we have learned to see our failure and learn from it. An apparent realism of universal sinfulness runs through theology, preaching and church language and makes everything seem grey on grey.

But this is where all revolutionary experiences begin: people are in God's field of power and only from there can their actions also be good. Mark stated this quite clearly by mentioning the *dynamis*, the power of God to the one who believes and trusts. This emerges in Luther in his discovery that human beings are made good and just: '... our works do not make us good, but our goodness, indeed even more the goodness of God makes us and our works good'.[4]

I can see this today in the way God is experienced by a black woman to whom the writer Alice Walker gives the following remarks: 'But once we feel loved by God, us do the best us can to please him with what us like.' And when her friend Celie anxiously asks, 'You telling me God love you, and you ain't never done nothing for him? I mean, not go to church, sing in the choir, feed the preacher and all like that?', she replies: 'But if God love me, Celie, I don't have to do all that. Unless I want to. There's a lot of other things I can do that I speck God likes... I can simply sit back and wonder at things. Be happy. Be beautiful.'⁵

This being good is not a moral quality. It means our being, our existence, which is right, justified, legitimate and full of quality. So 'I am good' primarily means, 'I am good as I am'. Or in theological language: I am made by God, for pleasure, I am loved, freed.

And it follows from this that I also act in this power of God, in the power of this goodness. A good tree brings forth good fruits.

So our being precedes our action: 'We are not righteous through doing right things, but because we are righteous we do right things.'⁶ I am not what I am through what I do. I am not good because I do good, but I do good because I am good.

But what does 'being good' look like for women in our culture?

Good is a very ambivalent word. We should all be good, good intentioned: that was the advice of our elders, above all of our mothers, and from an early age 'being a good girl' gave us an apparently good conscience and social recognition. The good child then had to become the good wife and the good mother – even now husbands and children attach considerable importance to this! However, 'become' is an exaggeration. The important thing was to remain in this state of being good, this childish, unaggressive, unassuming state of simply being there, which moved over smoothly from being adapted to adults to being adapted to husband and children. (There is also something formless and shapeless behind the term 'a good husband', which is not used very often.)

Women still have easier access to being good, meaning gracious and understanding. Many people have wanted this and continue to want it. Only the permanent failure of such basic goodness raises the question whether this goal is not too high or wide of the mark.

In our competitive social culture these origins, the basic feeling of being good, have been lost. For many women – according to the comments of a woman psychologist at a city clinic for nervous disorders – 'guilt feelings are the basic problem of woman's existence'.[7] Women excuse themselves, explain, ask for understanding far more often than men, and seek the causes of all ill primarily in themselves. 'Even in my early childhood years I learned to know the feeling of guilt,' a woman recalls. 'I felt so guilty when I defended myself. And I think that as an adolescent girl I was extremely rebellious.'- Luise Rinser recalls: 'All my education was aimed at making me quiet and biddable, lying low, always having a guilt feeling which cannot be put into words, always having to ask for pardon.'[8] Women can only experience the gospel of acceptance through God when this basic feeling of guilt is removed, swept aside, worked through. But anyone who reflects on justification today must take this diffuse basic feeling of feminine guilt into account and come to terms with it. It is false guilt, and we must become aware that it is, and it is ultimately guilt which stands between women and the God who makes his sun shine on everyone, who wants to make his powers visible in this world through human beings. Without this reflection we shall never experience afresh the nature of liberation and real forgiveness of actual guilt.

The other side of the coin of the diffuse feminine feeling of guilt is that women must make much greater efforts to stand up for themselves and for others, They must justify themselves through actions, demonstrate their right to exist and make themselves indispensable.

If we follow the old wisdom that newness, new good deeds only come from a new being, we must put aside our anxiety at quietistic passiveness and activist super-achievement and ask where our being is. Do we not constantly mistrust our being and have we not already been told that our being is good?

Putting our being before our actions first means understanding, grasping what our being is, and replacing our accustomed and inbred mistrust of ourselves with trust in ourselves. It also means being detached from our activities and learning the pain of being dispensable.

On this basis of trust we can then give up internalized mistrust of our action, our hyper-activity and our passivity. In an investigation of Tillich's and Niebuhr's understanding of justification Judith Plaskow wonders: 'Perhaps a doctrine of justification can develop which takes account of failure to become a self and opens up a process of self-actualization... Perhaps we must become somewhat Pelagian (playing our part in salvation) in order to do justice to women's experience.'[9]

Here the traditional doctrine of justification leaves us in the lurch. Even in its modern form, it has never been applied to women and worked out in terms of their own selves. 'I am good' must be supplemented by the affirmation 'I am whole'. Being whole already contains a characteristic element of our selves.

I am whole

For many theologians, wholeness belongs in the sphere of fable, but the longing for wholeness permeates all the women's religious literature of the nineteenth and twentieth centuries.[10] What do we understand by it today? What is wholeness for women? And what relation does it have to our being accepted?

After a somewhat tense conversation about questions of faith in a women's group, the suggestion was made that people should talk about wholeness. It was fascinating to see the personal and lively way in which women could speak about it:

For one it was the experience of an African night under the stars of a southern sky.

For another it was the hour after the birth of her first child.

A third detected wholeness in informal conversation with her pupils after the lesson.

157

These different spontaneous descriptions reflected the personalities, the fantasies, the dreams and the situations of those who gave them. They could express what they detected, felt, though they could not talk about faith adequately, or found it painful to put into words. And so there was no bridge between faith and wholeness.

In our culture 'faith' is too overloaded with dogma, is communicated in too one-sided a way with words and rationalized through discussions. Faith as it is spoken of in the New Testament and above all in the stories of Jesus affects other senses than hearing: smell, feeling, touch. Matter, wine, oil are experienced in it. Anxiety about natural theology has blunted our senses, has excluded nose, eye and skin and left only the ear. If we are again to grasp the whole God we shall again have to use all our organs. We must taste, see and feel how gracious the Lord is – not just through wine and offerings.

For me, being whole means three things:

1. Living from all the senses. The experiences of the senses: introducing colours, smells, feelings into experiences of faith and of God. Anything which is devoid of the senses soon also becomes senseless.

2. Accepting the allegedly inferior parts of my person and integrating them. What we have learned in psychology to be the 'lower' parts of our personality are part and parcel of us. However, we must ask whether these 'dark' sides, these 'shadows', do not come from a male perspective in which these sides are devalued because they are regarded as base and therefore too controlling. And the conviction is growing among women that these parts belong to us and make up our personality: our passions, our rage, our feelings, our aggressions. Someone who feels pain must cry out in this pain. However inappropriate it may seem to us, anger is part of the picture, for without it we would tone down ourselves and our development. We are whole, i.e. we are not balanced personalities whose supreme good is harmony.

In a balanced rational culture women have learned to adapt

to patriarchal values. They hide and conceal what does not fit in, but now and then it bursts out from them spontaneously, though with feelings of shame and guilt:

I am too spontaneous.

I always exaggerate.

I am hysterical.

I am too emotional.

These are usually charges which they have heard about themselves. But as e.g. Marianne Schuller has noted, hysteria 'is the name for a process of exclusion constitutive of femininity'. The hysterical woman is stamped into the ground in the name of a philosophical concept of subject in a male mould, because she is not one. She is characterized 'by a rejection of a male organization of wishes which has a genital stamp'.[11]

Women are beginning to reject such definitions and assertions which at an earlier stage goaded them to react coolly, in a predominantly rational way, and always to the point. Since they have become aware of themselves and the fact that they understand with the body,[12] aware that thought comes from imagination, that passion is part of our actions, that women have an overall comprehension, they are deliberately beginning to establish new values. They are clear that they can both think logically and grasp in an integrative way. They are aware of their progress, their flexible capacities, even if so far they can determine the style in public only in the narrowest circles. Nevertheless they often still feel themselves to be deviants from the norm, and self-acceptance is a laborious and painful process.

We only become whole when we regain the capacities which have been taken from us, rediscover wholeness and the fascinating awareness of our feelings, when we bring back into play the instinct that we hardly use. In this way we shall come up against many fragments and broken parts of ourselves which we can hardly knit together, but we shall again win back, yes win back, an element of originality, gain a possession, love, cherish. We who are still accustomed to let ourselves fall into pieces need this distinctive feature so that we feel good and right instead of experiencing ourselves as a deviation from the norm. Being whole means that we do not have to be perfect. Because I am whole I no longer need to be perfect: this perfidious substitute which we have put in the place of wholeness.

3. If I am whole, become whole, become body, feel body and live in a physical way, I can again feel nature and rediscover the earth. In this way domination of nature within me and outside myself can become friendship.

This is not a slippery retreat into an apparent harmony with the universe. On the contrary, it provokes conflicts, for if I am whole I suffer from the fact that creation is not whole and have the right and the duty to protest that this creation is no longer whole. By being whole we are involved in conflicts which shape our lives.

But in the long run we can only maintain this 'style of friendship' which will bring us into conflict with all styles of domination if we perceive God in a different way and speak of him other than as lord, king, judge. We shall have to discover God again with all our senses and capacities as Being, who grasps our being and precedes it.

'God love all them feelings,' says the black writer Alice Walker. 'That's some of the best stuff God made. And when you know that God loves 'em you enjoy them a lot more.'[13]

I am beautiful

When the black population in the USA carried on their fight for equal rights, a slogan emerged which was to reverse the deeply internalized sense of inferiority, of being black, dark, of less value: Black is beautiful. I was reminded of this phrase when there was a discussion in a women's group about what it is to accept oneself. None of the women could really accept themselves from top to toe, with what they felt to be good and what they felt to be bad, inside and out, with charm and physical flaws. There remained external things which women hated or had learned to hate in themselves: 'the weaknesses' – a typical conception orientated on 'strength', which is a false criterion; the 'mistake', a pedagogical norm which is developed over against the questionable model of correctness; the 'wrong sort' of beauty, a deficiency measured by the ideals of beauty held by males; the 'quirks', the crazy deviations from the norm of usual conduct which makes us fools, different, outsiders, abnormal. What they had learned to fight – the weaknesses, the faults, the quirks – remained external. Acceptance or justification is socially conditioned and depends on our social and anthopological presuppositions. Others have determined what is inferior.

We must change our thinking and learn to change our lives. But as long as we are dependent on the norms and their prejudices, as long as we do not live in a sovereign way on the basis of new values, we must survive in these norms. What we need here is a fascinating, transforming, creative feeling of self, of being beautiful – over against all the opinions and experiences which we encounter. Our mothers wanted us to be beautiful, a reflection of the unfulfilled self of their dreams, a point of attraction for future husbands. Beautiful in our own individual way, which does not correspond to current ideals of beauty, we were not so keen, and their dreams – which we hardly fulfilled, if at all – are still before our eyes and hang round our necks.

It is difficult to find ourselves beautiful because we were not allowed to become beautiful. We only become beautiful when someone finds us beautiful. The young Luther said that 'Sinners are beautiful because they are loved',[14] and in so doing introduced something of the transforming love of God. Children and people become beautiful only if we find them beautiful. But we can only find them beautiful if we ultimately find ourselves beautiful. And this reciprocal relationship shapes all human relationships. How can we break through the vicious circle? How can we accept ourselves in our deepest being?

If we try the game of looking at the personal side that we feel to be negative and turning it round, the vicious circle can be broken, and self-love can arise out of self-hatred. 'I am so emotional,' a woman recently lamented in tears when she was working in a YMCA group – dominated by males. If the woman understands that this emotionalism is part of her life and is an important, necessary contribution to this group, her feelings of guilt and anxiety will diminish. An important feature here will be for another woman to back her up and strengthen her.

When reversed and traced back to their origins, what we have come to learn and hate as typical female characteristics, like talkativeness or pettiness, become a passionate interest in the little things of everyday life and the capacity to talk to people and help children to talk. Speech is life-giving, everyday work is the support to the basis of life. Elevated silence, 'essential', significant words could hardly have created the communication from which life comes.

Women sometimes have difficulties with male 'logic'. Their grasshopper logic is mocked and silenced. However, it has a capacity to grasp more things, and more important things, to be apt and imaginative. If it is accepted for what it is, the 'other' logical capacities often develop out of it. The psychoanalyst Jean Baker Miller speaks of the strength of feminine weaknesses and shows that what women did and how they lived created a value system which was never recognized and rewarded:

...in the past it was left to women to deal creatively with the psyche, with the life of the human soul. That means that the women in a society which denied them the properties it prized most had to develop a certain inner awareness of what it means to be a valuable person, though in that case this awareness did not correspond with the supreme values of society. Thus traditionally the woman had largely to transform for example the social values in her own awareness in order to arrive at the conviction that the furthering of the development of other people would strengthen her own awareness as a person... In this sense women who led a traditional life have built up a progressive inner and therefore authentic value system.[15]

In present times it has become necessary to bring this value system out into the open and to see where we can open out this hidden women's culture and introduce it again.

If women stop adapting themselves to a closed system, whether of the church or of society, in order to be accepted, then we shall have the beginnings of a change.

If we find ourselves beautiful, turn self-hatred into self-love, our weaknesses become strengths.

I can give vent to my repressed feelings.

My darker side becomes meaningful for me and my person, indeed becomes the basic substance of my personality.

What I have suppressed breaks out in a creative way.

My quirks become charms.

If I find myself beautiful, I shall not remain narcissistically in love with myself. If I find myself beautiful I shall also find other things and other people beautiful and attractive. If I stop being anxious about and hostile to my 'dark' side, I shall stop being anxious about others and aggressive towards them. In that case anxiety at what is strange, unclear and devalued will turn into amazement at what is alien, curiosity about what is unknown. Then I shall find dark and negative things atractive. Then I shall be able to love anew.

The vicious circle in which we transfer our own small and anxious ego to others can be broken through in this way. If a woman permanently looks for her guilt in herself, she will primarily seek its cause in the failure of another woman. For instance, if her neighbour has a marital crisis, she will make the woman the responsible party. If she has freed herself from attributions of guilt she will also be freer towards other women. We assess the world by our own standards. It ultimately depends on the self-love which makes us beautiful whether we change anything in the world.

This love of the neighbour which arises from self-love and self-acceptance does not take over the other person. Nor does it make up his or her mind. It leaves the other free, with the patience which we allow ourselves.

Something else emerges from our being beautiful. We no longer need lightning conductors for our anxieties and aggressions. We no longer need to project the guilt with which we cannot cope on to others – on to men, churches and societies. We become 'I', we create an 'I', which stands by itself and which is responsible for ourselves.

Many women today seek a theology which makes them guiltless. This shows how oppressive and burdensome the gospel of human liberation has seemed. It contains the offer that we need no longer experience guilt as the basic ill of our existence. We shall continue to be guilty. But we can learn and develop more skill in recognizing real guilt, in confronting it as whole persons, in seeing through our motives and our actions better and in charming away the feminine guilt in ourselves and among us with the charm of self-love, which tells us that we are good, whole and beautiful. In doing this we are not creating illusions but reality, which is as real as we depict it.

The American Valerie Saiving Goldstein has spoken of 'female sin' as the 'underdevelopment or negation of the I'. In contrast to the male sin of hybris, wanting to be like God, women are alienated from themselves and from God in that they cannot be themselves.[16] They are not the perfect ones, the only true believers. In Mark they flee (16.8), are weak and suddenly afraid when they no longer find Jesus and are to proclaim the resurrection of Jesus. The sin of women is that they no longer tolerate the risk of 'I am', long for continuity and leave the narrow way of autonomy from which our relationships first develop – that they stick in a group, are choked by a bond, lose themselves in some form of solidarity,

In the acceptance and self-acceptance described here this anxiety which makes us small, this separation from God, is done away with. The prodigal daughter of God is the one who returns to herself, to the fatherly arms of God who is our mother. This acceptance can be experienced, promised and felt. It can come from outside, and it can be self-acceptance. The christological *extra nos* which is so important for the traditional doctrine of justification has shifted somewhat in the experience of women. The women were and are those who look on (*theorein*), which at the same time means accept the story of Jesus in themselves and become like him. They bear his message in their bodies, in themselves, and thus do away with the division between inside and outside. The searching test that this can prove is shown by their flight in Mark and by our own experience of ourselves. Nevertheless, the confidence that it can give is shown by the common experience of all Christians which Paul has expressed as:'If anyone is in Christ there is a new creation. The old has passed away. Behold, all has been made new' (II Cor.5.17).

Mediaeval devotional picture of St Anne. Altar in Niederlana.
Hans Schnatterpeck, between 1503 and 1510

11

PATRIARCHAL AND MATRIARCHAL LOVE

> Love is ridiculous
> It rides on a donkey
> on clothes strewn in the way
> One can hail it
> crown it with thorns
> and make short shrift of it
> It seeks a refuge in the muzzles of our guns
> A celebrated case
> the proceedings
> are still in the balance.
>
> *Eva Zeller*

The love of Sophia

The background to this mutual use of power, confidence and trust and its possibility is the unconditional approach, described above, of the Sophia of God as it is proclaimed by the Sermon on the Mount and the parables, and as it is experienced in the table-fellowship of Jesus with the publicans, the outcast and outsiders.[1] In the New Testament letters and in John we find the central concept of love – agape – to express it.

However, in the Synoptic Gospels the noun love occurs only in two passages (Matt.24.12; Luke 11.42), and even there not with any evocative significance. The verb love (*agapan*) without an object appears in the story of the woman who was a sinner: she loved much (Luke 7.47); it occurs often with an object, the neighbour, the enemy, God the Lord. These love commandments for men and women have a central place in the message of the Synoptic Gospels. However, the concept of the love of God is absent here. All the more impressive, then, is the way in which this turning towards God, this love, is described in the first three Gospels: the father who accepts his prodigal son unconditionally; the woman who looks for her lost penny as though it were a golden treasure; the employer who pays all his workers the same wage.

The characteristic of this approach is that it applies to everyone. It not only transcends classes, races and sexes but overthrows all our scales of value. God, who in our language is so closely associated with the good, loses his moral aspect. He is also a God of the scoundrels. He is the God who makes his sun shine on bad and good alike and the rain fall on the just and the unjust (Matt.5.45). This also has connections with the Old Testament scale of values: the decision which is set before human beings relating to good and evil has no ultimate validity for this God (Deut.30.15).

This 'immoral' God of the plebeians and aristocrats, the wrecks and the whole, those who do harm and those who do good, bursts through all moral categories. He can only be grasped in conceptuality drawn from nature. S/he is like the sun and the rain, which cannot be avoided: 'the sun also rises on criminals and the seas are open to pirates,' laments Seneca.[2] S/he is like the mother who gives life and accepts the newborn baby regardless of whether it is ugly or beautiful, reacts gratefully or with indifference. Since God looks on everyone in the same way, makes them the same, he arouses our capacity to love ourselves and in this way to accept one another: 'Love your neighbour as yourself.' In addition,this God also opens up a sphere to evil in which the evil must not be annihilated: 'Do not resist evil.' It is the sphere of non-violence, which opens up for those who live under this sovereignty of the Sophia God.

In the Sermon on the Mount we have an authentic encounter with the experience of this bias towards us and its personal and social consequences. Its consequences are a confidence in oneself and the other which makes solidarity and equality possible. The new community is brought together through the energies of the matriarchal God. Discipleship – a word misused in an ascetic sense and often misunderstood – is not an act of obedience but the organic consequence of the dynamic of this community. Apparatus for threats and punishment is inconceivable here. However, this turning of God can also be rejected, and not accepted. The death of Jesus is the brutal consequence of this rejection in wisdom theology.

This agape is seen as the centre of Christianity. It is the basic Christian motive before all others. The noun agape is regarded as 'a quite new creation of Christianity'.[3] Without this motive, it is said, Christianity would lose its character. However, in my view a hitherto unseen matriarchal origin can be assumed. In the Greek sphere, *agapan* in pre-Christian times certainly seemed insignificant and banal. 'In the word *agapan* the Greek finds nothing of the power and magic of *eran* and little of the warmth of *philein*... its meaning is weak and variable.'[4] It is not heroic but rather used in an everyday, human way to denote respect and fellow feeling between those of equal status, signs of friendship and love which are given to others. However, we also encounter *agape* (*agapan*) as a cult name of Isis in a long ancient Isis liturgy which was discovered in the second century AD,[5] and we find the phrase 'beloved of Isis'.[6] This basic Christian motive is perhaps not a new coining on the part of Christians but may also have had a Sitz im Leben in the life of the Isis cult – specifically in its everyday nature and humanity.

In terms of the psychology of religion too, this love is matriarchal love. Since Johann Jakob Bachofen investigated early cultures and religions in the last century and discovered in matriarchal cultures this love which gives itself unconditionally to strangers,[7] we have learned to distinguish between matriarchal and patriarchal love. According to Erich Fromm 'the essence of paternal love' consists in imposing demands, establishing laws and making love for the son dependent on his obeying orders.

By contrast a mother's love is 'the unconditional affirmation of the child's life and his needs... It is the attitude which instils in the child a love for living, which gives him the feeling: it is good to be alive.' There are two aspects to this maternal love: on the one hand it arouses the will to live and on the other it awakens the feeling that it is good to be alive.[8] However, it is in no way limited to the mother! Mothers brought up to the norms of patriarchy can also love in a 'patriarchal' way, their love depending on good behaviour, social norms, the child's achievement. Fathers can love and accept just as unconditionally – like the father of the prodigal son. In many respects the love of God which Jesus demonstrates in actions and in narratives has clear relationships to the traditions of women.

But this matriarchal agape which in Christianity becomes the basic concept for God's way of dealing with humanity develops a shadowy side, and we still suffer under the shadow: it is made hierarchical and robbed of its friendly, sisterly character. For many people this Christian love has meanwhile become a concept which is intolerably misused and worn out. They see 'love' embodied in and subordinated to structures which are hostile to life, or they experience it as a fatal 'patriarchalism of love',[9] that apparent relaxation of a fixed order which is nevertheless in the last resort a betrayal of the cause of Jesus and a perversion of its original content.

I would like to give three examples to show how the original, all-embracing and radical character of love changed.

The patriarchy of love

This unconditional love has already disappeared from the instructions to households on leading a good and Christian life. Granted, at the beginning of the admonitions about marriage in Ephesians it is said that all should be subject to one another in the fear of the Lord. However, immediately after that the equal terma are amended: wives are further commended to be specially subordinate to their husbands;

PATRIARCHAL AND MATRIARCHAL LOVE

'Wives should be subordinate to their husbands in the Lord' (5.22). The model for this is Christ and the community. That indeed is the theme of Ephesians, and the picture of the body and the head comes from this. Just as Christ is the head and the community is the body, so the husband is the head and the wife is the body. The two belong indissolubly together. However, the activity begins from the head. As Christ loves his community so the husband is to love the wife.

The command to love one's neighbour from the Sermon on the Mount serves as a clarification: 'Even so husbands should love their wives as their own bodies. He who loves his wife loves himself' (v.28). 'Let each of you love his wife as himself' (v.33).

The patriarchal order of marriage is thus relaxed, humanized, Christianized by the commandment to love. The love of Jesus for human beings is the example from which married love is derived. This had its function and its historical significance for rigid structures of order. However, this concept remained incomplete because the object of love, the wife, could not equally be invited to love. She remains passive, is body, is compared with 'flesh'. What is left for her to do is to subordinate herself and fear her husband: 'Let each one of you love his wife as himself, but let the wife fear her husband' (v.33).

The flow of love goes one-sidedly from the head, from the man, from Christ. There is no longer mutuality. The patriarchal order is not changed, but at most penetrated. The revolutionary potential of love was wasted.

For almost two thousand years the 'patriarchalism of love' remained the form in which the original agape was constricted and embodied. At the same time this made men feel that they were the authentic vehicles of this love while women had to wait for it passively, receptively, gratefully and modestly. There was no provision for them to let this love become creative, to shape themselves in the light of their own experience of it.

From God's love to love of God

However, a second shift can be noted in the New Testament: if in the Synoptic Gospels men and women are the subject of agape, in that they are summoned and encouraged to love themselves, their neighbour and God; if in Luke the woman who was a sinner can even be a kind of model of spontaneous, unmotivated, self-sacrificing love; in Paul human beings now lose the capacity to be the subject of the agape of God.

In this section I shall use the researches of Anders Nygren, who here – more unconsciously – gives a good description of male experience and male thought, using Paul as an example.[10]

According to Nygren the idea of agape is rooted in the religious development of Paul's life. The persecutor has become a disciple and apostle. He does not feel worthy (I Cor.15.9), sees himself as 'one born out of time' (v.8). This experience revealed to him 'the ways of God. It gave him an insight into God's agape and Christ's agape, it showed him the absolutely unmotivated character of God's love.' From this it follows for Paul that there is no way from human beings to God. The old world order, according to which there is a way to God through the law, has been thrown out. 'A transvaluation took place that put a different complexion on everything.' A new set of values was given; by receiving God's call and election in his greatest sin Paul experienced that 'That is agape, that is God's way to man.'

From now on his theology is stamped by the experience that there is no wày from humanity to God, but only a way from God to humanity. Nothing comes from humanity. The reality of agape which he found in the traditions of the community and which clearly appears in the Synoptic Gospels as a basic Christian theme, now becomes a central theme for him: agape becomes the technical term for his theology. From the experience of his own guilt and experience of love agape and the theology of the cross now coincide for him: God shows his agape to us by the fact that Christ died for us while we were still sinners (Rom.5.8).

Agape is manifested only in the death of Jesus on the cross. Only God is the subject of this agape. Something absolutely spontaneous and unmotivated in God appears here: for who dies for sinners? And this is even true for those who are remote from God, the atheists.

If in all religions human sacrifice is needed to reconcile God (and bad consciences) – sacrificial offerings in primitive religions, obedience and humility in more sublimated stages – by contrast for Paul all human ways to God are now transcended: the sacrifice is God's own sacrifice. 'Sacrifice is no longer man's way to God but God's way to man.' According to Nygren, here Jesus' gospel of the fatherly love of God has undergone a far-reaching development.

Since agape in Paul finds its basis and centre in God, central statements about the love of humanity for God – which can still be found in the Synoptic Gospels – are missing. Love for the neighbour has remained, and remained central. However human beings are only capable of this horizontal love, not of vertical love. The twofold commandment of love has lost a dimension.

Nygren sees here in Paul a climax in the history of agape thinking:

If agape is a love as absolutely spontaneous and entirely unmotivated as the love manifested in the cross of Jesus, then it is plain that the word agape can no longer fittingly be used as a designation to denote man's attitude to God. In relation to God, man is never spontaneous. He is not a centre of activity. His giving of himself to God is never more than a response. At its best and highest it is but a reflex of God's love, by which it is 'motivated'. Hence it is the very opposite of spontaneous and creative...

Therefore human surrender to God must seek another

name. The place of agape is taken by *pistis* – faith. It is love, but with the character of receptiveness, not spontaneity.

But since agape is purely theocentric, it also loses the capacity for being self-love. Agape does not seek its own (I Cor.13.5). This incomprehensible agape out of which God sacrifices his Son can no longer be predicated of human beings oppressed by guilt. It can certainly be poured by the Holy Spirit into human hearts (Rom.5.5), but the subject is no longer humanity but God, his spirit, his love. In I Cor.13 humanity again seems to be the centre of love, but this is a description of the divine power of agape. 'An outflow from God's own life... Here the question no longer arises whether agape is love to God or love to one's neighbour. It is just simply agape, the life of agape shining its own light, regardless of any significance it might acquire from its object.'

Loss of radical love

In Paul we have a typical piece of male theorizing. A personal experience is made the basis for a universally valid theory; his own experience of guilt becomes experience of God. The personal experience of conflict serves to support general statements about the *humanum*: e.g. that there is no creative spontaeous love of God, that human nature in relationship to God is only reflex, receptivity, and that human beings have no independent centre in themselves.

Moreover this is a piece of male theologizing: because experience of God is defined in terms of Paul's experience of guilt, God becomes remote, unapproachable, separated from guilty humanity by a deep divide. The unconditional love of the Sophia God, the love which treats all equally and without distinction, which calls forth spontaneity and derives from spontaneity, loses its dynamism and mutuality. God becomes the centre and starting point of love. The love of man for God and for oneself which lies at the heart of the gospel is removed. God loses his nearness and becomes unattainable. The brutal death of Jesus caused by human beings becomes the sacrificial death for the sin of humanity, a sacrifice allowed by the transcendent God. Just as he becomes the sole subject of agape, so too he becomes the subject of this offering. God, the absolute, becomes the source of all incomprehensible love, but even in his aloofness he remains the cause for all incomprehensible events.

In the Synoptic Gospels the surrender of Jesus, the betrayal, is still clearly attributed to Judas (Matt.26.15). In Paul the same event is raised to a higher plane: God the author of agape becomes the author of the surrender of his Son (Rom.8.32). This paradox seems to me still to contain elements of a punitive God who requires satisfaction, which no longer have any connection with the Sophia God. God's radical love remains conditioned in Paul; it does not change God radically – a piece of the patriarchal image of God, something of the old God of anxiety, remains.

Paul reflected on the appearance of 'unconditional love' from the perspective of his experience of guilt: the transcendence of all guilt, a revolutionary new experience of God which at the same time would also remove all religious boundaries. However, this did not take in his hierarchical thinking and an ascetic hostility to the body. Many people found and still find their own experience reflected in his. But the history of women, the other history of companionship, contemporaneity, compassion, did not become evident there; indeed it was repressed. God was no longer present in the experiences of the women by the cross and at Easter. Their new pattern of mutuality did not become established. This was not only a theological difference but also had social dimensions and perhaps also a social cause: the hierarchical pattern of man = humanity in Paul corresponded to his social model of man – wife; both were fundamentally unaffected, and all the modifications brought about through love could not repair the loss of radical love.

Research into the psychology of development (e.g. by

Carol Gilligan) has now drawn our attention to the forms of perception in women which are different from those in men, and of which theology should also take account.

> The failure to see the different reality of women's lives and to hear the differences in their voices stems in art from the assumption that there is a single mode of social experience and interpretation. By positing instead two different modes we arrive at a more complex rendition of human experience which sees the truth of separation and attachment in the lives of women and men and recognizes how these truths are carried by a different mode of thought and language.'[11]

If one side dominates, the result must inevitably be caricatures of reality and wrong ideas of life and salvation.

The idea of an atoning sacrifice, which also appears in Paul, but hardly in the New Testament, and develops all the more strongly in the later traditions, has nothing to do with the original significance and interpretation of the death of Jesus. It is an attempt to connect the God who calls for satisfaction with the unconditional love that is experienced in Christ, to get a grip on matters, to interpret the incomprehensible, guilt-laden death of Jesus with known religious conceptions. But by doing this one at the same time escapes the radical nature and the involvement. The mutuality and challenge of love are lost. The personal and social consequences of the love command-ment are only retained in a broken way. The sacrificial death becomes a distant model which can hardly be accomplished every day, and which could be used by particular societies as an incitement towards the final sacrifice or even to transfigure it, e.g. in times of war.

'Sacrifice' as an ethical model also had a similar transfiguring role for women: mothers allegedly 'sacrificed' themselves for their children, and 'sacrificed' their sons for the fatherland. They even 'sacrificed' their family, others, their husband and his career. But in so far as women identified with this sacrificial theory they throttled rebellion and their own experience. Is not a mother's love fundamentally part of her identity which is taken for granted and which pours out naturally, but is now idealized as sacrifice? Is brutality in war, which is meant to be excused and made tolerable with the 'sacrifice' of mothers, not an absurd attack on life and a diversion of the really vital interests of a mother? Was the mother's sacrifice, programmed at all times as a dissolution into a self-dissolution, which did not destroy others, crowned with an exalted image?

The sacrifice and love of Jesus, torn from the relationships of those who surrounded him, handed over to the heads, the existential experiences, the existential anxeties of men, lost its dynamics. It lost its eroticism and its dimensions of friendship. It was imprisoned in a cult, embodied in a male and used in order to maintain structures, to interpret meaninglessness meaningfully and to motivate readiness for sacrifice.

However, there are experiences of limitation and loneliness where there is guilt which cannot be overcome, where there is no longer any companionship, where love and surrender to Jesus are still experienced as vicarious. Here the idea of 'sacrifice' can take on a comforting significance, without involving tormented images of God and images of sacrifice.

The pedagogy of patriarchal love

In 1904 a child's book appeared by Agnes Sapper called *Die Familie Pfäffling*. The last edition was published in 1966 (bringing the total copies printed to 750,000) and can still be bought in bookshops, and it is probably one of the most-read children's books.[12] It depicts the domestic life of the large family of a Christian music teacher in Swabia. The parents are not pedagogical extremists, but show how ordinary everyday conflicts were resolved at the time, and the fact that the book has survived for eighty years shows how relevant this pedagogy is still thought to be. One scene gives a particularly impressive picture of patriarchal love: the small son Frieder, who is very musical, has been given a violin which he loves more than anything in the world. He may practise on it for three hours a day, but no more. One day his enthusiasm gets the better of him. He is told to stop, but he just cannot stop playing. His mother says to him, 'So you knew that it was past the time and you went on playing? I wouldn't have thought that of you, Frieder; if you forget to obey over your violin it's probably better for your violin playing to stop altogether. Stay here and I will hear what father thinks.'

When his father comes, Frieder makes excuses. 'I'm sorry.' But that does not satisfy the father. 'Of course you must be sorry,' he says. 'If you had just forgotten that you had played over time through excitement, I could easily have forgiven you, but if you remembered that you should have stopped and went on, if you deliberately did what I have often forbidden you to do, then that's the end of violin playing... my children must obey, and that's the end of your violin playing – I will not say for ever, but for a year and a day.'

But Frieder cannot part with his violin, He hugs it to himself and will not give it up for anything. Then his father says, 'All right, keep your violin, and here's a bow as well. You can play as long as you like. But you are only our child when you give it to us.' And opening the door into the courtyard he calls out in a threatening way, 'Get out, strange child.' And he tells the domestic servant, 'The child is to stay there like a poor beggar child. He may remain outside here at the front; he may have food, and at night you can give him a cushion to sleep on. Give him the kitchen stool to sit on... because he no longer has a father or a mother.' And he says to the family, 'Hunger shall not drive him to us, but love and conscience.' But what love will come out of this? What love will restore the small child to the father?

What Father Pfäffling practises here is what the psychologists of religion call patriarchal love.

The nature of fatherly love is that he makes demands, establishes principles and laws; his love for the son depends on the obedience of the latter to these demands. He likes best the son who is most like him, who is obedient and who is best fitted to become his successor, as the inheritor of his possessions.[13]

This love is caught up in the conceptions and wishes of the father. As supreme head he embodies a group, a society, the family. It calls for subordination, obedience. It does not pour out, it does not bring any awakening. It produces subjection and self-destruction, but it does not create mutuality.

Now in the Pfäffling story, significantly two women end this absurd situation. Whereas the mother – with unease yet without protest – hopes that all will be come right, but subordinates herself completely to the supreme head of the family, Frieder's twin sisters have the idea of ending this power struggle, though at their brother's expense and in favour of the patriarch. They cover the violin with a shawl as though with a shroud and Frieder is now in a position to return it to his father. The father's will is fulfilled. Frieder is now again his child, but something has been destroyed, broken, and the one whose will was broken will pass the effects on to the next generation.

The love experienced by the prodigal son did not become an adequate pedagogical possibility in the Christian West. It did not become a creative power for human relationships. And women, who were more aware of that, had learned to compensate but not to protest. As early as 1960 the American theologian Valerie S. Goldstein wrote: 'Contemporary theological doctrines of love have, I believe, been constructed primarily on the basis of masculine experience and thus view the human condition from the male standpoint. Consequently these doctrines do not provide an appropriate interpretation of the situation of women – nor, for that matter, of men, in view of certain fundamental changes now taking place in our society.'[14] Where are our models of love, which accord with our common human situation?

The holy women at the tomb. Mozac cathedral, twelfth century

12

MODELS FOR WOMEN

The kingdom of mothers is always of this world.

Ernest Borneman

Trinities

Can the Christian tradition today still offer helpful, humane, alternative models?

Our current basic ideas and images are being put in question from two sides, those of psychotherapy and feminism, and both sides doubt whether there are other pictures. For Horst Eberhard Richter there are hierarchical patterns of behaviour which are deeply rooted in our psyche.

'Compared with the traditional asymmetrical-hierarchical primal images of the loving relationships between God and creature, parents and child, dominating husband and dominated wife, giving Samaritan and receiving sufferer, the counterpart model of a love from like to like is not yet deeply anchored in imagery.'[1] If the domination of the woman is for Richter a symptom of the disruption of human relationships, for Mary Daly the suppression of the woman from all symbols is the cause of the self-destruction of the world. The unholy Trinity – war, violence and genocide – is a product of the Christian patriarchate. The thought-pattern in terms of omnipotence, transcendence and domination derived from one-sided male experience. In the last resort they are all rooted in the Christian symbol of the patriarchal Trinity:

The thought of Western society is still possessed overtly and subliminally by christian symbolism, and this State of

181

Possession has extended its influence over most of the planet. Its ultimate symbol of processions is the all-male Trinity itself. Of obvious significance here is the fact that this is an image of a divine son from a divine father (no mother or daughter is involved). In this symbol the first person, the father, is the origin, thinks forth the second person, the son, the word of himself, who is the perfect image... So total is their union that their mutual love is expressed by the procession of a third person, the 'Holy Spirit'... This meaning of the three divine persons is the model for the pseudogeneric term person, excluding all female mythic presence, denying female reality in the cosmos.[2]

These examples from psychotherapy and radical feminism show how short of images we are and how impossible it is to arrive at new models which we urgently need for psychological and social survival. In fact our traditional Christianity with its patriarchal exegesis leaves us in the lurch. For Daly the consequence is that women are abandoning the church and phallic morality and going into the new territory of their own women's culture, which is no longer necrophilic. The way there is by means of iconoclasm – the destruction of all pre-existing oppressive images. Are we at the end of a culture, with no images, no ground to stand on? Must we create new images? But who will accept them, and how can they take on social significance?

Whereas with us this iconoclasm is still in full flood, for years American women theologians have been trying to discover the content of well-known Christian symbols and in so doing questioning whether the patriarchal hermeneutics of the Trinity have sole validity. The male Trinity has always been preceded in the history of religion by a female Trinity. Father, Son and Spirit are only an ill-concealed patriarchal model superimposed on the background of old myths. If in Germany the doctrine of the Trinity is still suspected of being a metaphysical speculation remote from life, in American interpretations there are indications of its psycho-social, ethical significance and the possibilities of finding new patterns of relationship in it.

In the context of process theology, for example, Marjorie Suchocki sees the possibility and necessity of ending the male trauma.

> When we loose the notion of 'trinity' from its sexist moorings we move beyond thinking of God simply as a human being larger-than-life... Trinitarian thought should force us beyond our usual human categories, asking us to intuit a manyness-in-unity far beyond our experience...[3]

Patricia Wilson Kastner sees in the trinitarian conception of perichoresis (dance, intermingling) of persons in the image of the dance a confirmation of feminist conceptions of relationships and mutuality in the most beautiful way.[4]

For Margaret Farley, too, the equality and mutuality of love is grounded in the Trinity: the first and the second persons are 'infinitely active and infinitely receptive, infinitely giving and infinitely receiving, holding in infinite mutuality and reciprocity a totally shared life'. As Farley knows how allergic women are to male symbolism, she suggests in accordance with modern biology, which also assigns the mother an active role, that the image of husband and wife should take the place of the earlier picture of father and son.[5]

However, there are also critical voices. There are traditional hesitations from the German side: 'I cannot (yet) understand how God can be made in the images of a mother-child binity, a mother-child-father triad, a transformed triadic doctrine of emanation' (Uwe Gerber).[6]

Barbara Hilkert Andolsen has fundamental doubts as to whether a religion which would include the feminine aspect of God would still be Christianity:

> It will be extraordinarily difficult for Christianity to embody

in its symbols a belief that women are full human beings and hence are equally capable of serving as symbols of divine power. Yet unless such fundamental changes in attitude towards women and towards ultimate power come about, it will not be possible to ground securely an ethic of mutuality in Christian religious dogmas.[7]

However, a glance at Christian tradition constantly shows feminine persons in conceptions of the Trinity (see the plate on p.104). Daly and indeed Farley and Hilkert-Andolsen do not go into this or they do not have a thorough knowledge of the theological traditions. In the history of the Christian churches the male Trinity has been continually disrupted by female components: Farley's conception of the Trinity as husband and wife already has a forerunner in the Coptic tradition: God and the holy Spirt are depicted as a married couple. Daly's wish for woman as the primal ground of all being has an original in art, in the 'self-disclosing Virgin' who carries Father and Son within her. These devotional images, which came into being above all in France and Germany in the fourteenth and fifteenth centuries, represent something like: in the beginning was the woman. They embody the idea that the gracious Trinity becomes incarnate in the body of the Mother of Mercy and has its effect from there. However, the heresy of deviation from the patriarchal schema soon became evident: around 1400 the French church teacher Jean Gerson, who stressed the boundless power of the arbitrariness in God, who also rejected the translation of the Bible into the vernacular and thought that it was better in the hands of bishops, criticized this kind of madonna as 'undevotion'. Thus it was impious to worship the maternal mercy as the being that encompasses us. Still allowed were the self-disclosing virgins who had only Jesus and the Holy Spirit within themselves, distanced God from a motherly origin and left room for God's arbitrariness.[8]

The social and theological background of such female incursions have so far been evident: almost always we can establish the power and influence of women. Women introduced themselves into a process from which they were excluded in mainstream culture.

Two purely female woman images give a particularly impressive representation of the capacity of women for relationships which are maintained through all patriarchal falsifications. They originally derive from a matriarchal context, have been preserved in an increasingly patriarchal Christianity and today stimulate our imagination for new dealings between women – and men.

Anna Selbdritt

Whereas a dual relationship expresses polarity and mutuality in a unity, the triad or the trinity is an image for a community with several dimensions, the image of all-embracing relationships. Three is the number of perfection, of infinity, the key to the universe.

One of these threefold relationships is the mother-daughter-child group which derives from matriarchal cultures: Demeter, Kore, Erechtheus. She represents the female genealogy, our maternal traditions, and she allows the child, the offshoot of this relationship, to develop. Here the father who begets, shapes and educates is unknown.

This matriarchal triad emerges above all in the art of the late Middle Ages as Anna Selbdritt (see the plate on p.166).[9] Mary with the child is joined by Anne, the mother of Mary. In pictures Anne is depicted as an older mature woman with a green cloak (hope) and a red garment (love); she has Mary beside her or on her lap or arm, while the child Jesus sits on Anne's other arm or in Mary's lap. Very often Anne – and sometimes also Mary – has a book in her hand. So she should be regarded as Mary's teacher.

Anne has no New Testament background. She is a legendary invention. However, when we investigate the needs from which legends arise, the reason is probably that the aetiological myth which first developed with Luke required that Mary should have an origin of her own. Anne appears as early as AD 150 and spreads through the East after 600 and in the West after 800; her cult exploded in the fifteenth and sixteenth centuries. At the same time and in the same areas where the Reformation spread, for example in the Mark of Brandenburg, a wealth of carved altars of St Anne appeared.

There are two sides to the origin of the cult of Anne. The upper side, expressed in church history and the history of dogma, says that growing conviction of the immaculate conception of Mary forced her legendary mother Anne into the foreground. It was then said of her that she had conceived Mary without desire, just through a kiss from her husband Joachim. At the Council of Basle in 1439 it was officially recommended that the Feast of the Immaculate Conception should be celebrated, and this was confirmed by Pope Sixtus in 1483, in three bulls.

The underside of the history has to be guessed at more than proved: to discover it we must begin from people and ask why this cult of Anne was accepted so intensively and became a fashion. Beda Kleinschmidt sees a special reason for the cult in its association with pregnancy and birth:

> ...in particular Anne, lovingly called mother, became a saint; according to legend she bore three children, and became a much invoked patroness of women who longed for the blessing of children or delighted in it. Women needed such a patron especially in a time like the end of the Middle Ages, which was so rich in children and which loved them so much.[10]

Mary, the primary Christian figure of the mother and wife, had apparently not been of use here. The historian Shulamith Shahar also observes with surprise that the figure of Mary hardly had any influence 'on the general picture of the mother who conceived and brought up her children in a natural way'.[11]

The glowing Mother of God and the wealth of grief which are depicted so richly did not communicate fundamental motherly properties like love and dedication. However, Anne fulfilled this role, which did not call for any unfulfillable ideal of sexual purity and virginity. There is something primal, sovereign, all-gracious about her. 'She always grants him what he requires of her,' said Celtis around 1500. And another enthused: 'Anyone who is in distress and calls in devotion to St Anne becomes restful and confident.'

The Greek bishop Petros of Argos affirmed her original matristic function in an increasingly patriarchal Christianity in a laudation around 900.

> Anne, as it were the beginning and the last sign of approaching redemption, saw the moon wane and that sun which exceeds all others in magnitude and splendour proceed from her own …
>
> Anne saw in herself not only an image but truth itself; she saw the primal image directly… She is the paradise of God which delighted us with the most glorious fruits of every kind. She is the field which gives of grain abundantly, the fruitful and nourishing earth…
>
> Anne is the true daughter of Abraham, but goes beyond him in praise…
>
> Thus Anne is exalted above all fathers and mothers, however much they may have wondered at her great praise as prophets and patriarchs.[12]

Anne remained a true mother, even if the church denied her desires and spiritualized her. She also led a real woman's life. According to legend she married three times and had children by three different husbands, who were said to be the three Maries. But here too the church sought to confine her to one marriage and to restrict excessive sexual life.

However, the matriarchal background of this Christian group is still very evident: Anne, the patroness of pregnant women, of grandmothers and widows, is above all also patroness of mountain people; she watches over ships and waters, and has to fulfil the functions of the great earth mother. On the underside of an Anna Selbdritt in St Jacob's Church, Nuremberg, an artist of the Veit-Stoss-workshop in 1505 depicted a moon as a symbol of the cosmos, the symbol of the goddess. So Anne's 'teaching book' is more than a book of wisdom, it is the original unity of knowledge and experience.

Anne was an earthy protest against late Gothic transcendental piety, which was worlds apart with its fragile, spiritualized Mary. She represents a new relationship of love and goodness between women and children.

Here a picture of piety came into being with which women could identify over many centuries. It showed them their worth, their significance for education and their involvement in a woman's culture. The child is not handed over to the mother nor the mother to the child. The third person, who is also necessary for the psychology of education, extends and relaxes the relationship. A man is not necessary. However, it is necessary for this person to embody book, knowledge, rationality, without stifling human relationships in emotionalism: a matriarchal love which dissolves neither mother nor child, but allows the formation of a person.

As a religious symbol this makes the image of the Father less fraught; it is a silent interpretation of the love of God which was nevertheless visible to the people. In this way underground traditions were expressed which have survived all patriarchal cultures and religions. Anna Selbdritt is a piece of women's history, women's knowledge, women's wisdom and women's relationships, and no matter how she might be interpreted and even used against women, she preserved some integrity and resistance.

The three women

At the very time that the carved Anne altars were spreading, another type of image was disappearing. This similarly trans-

MODELS FOR WOMEN

posed matriarchal traditions, but at the same time has a solid basis in the New Testament; it is the image of the three women (see the plate on p.180). Down to the fourteenth century, the representation of the three women at the tomb was regarded as the definitive Easter picture. The resurrection typology was subordinated to it in the West. The image introduced cycles of the appearance of the risen Christ or was the main way of depicting it.[13] In the second half of the fourteenth century, however, a new image of the resurrection appeared, which shows Jesus, the Christ, hovering over the grave. The two themes were combined again later in the following period. However, the Counter-Reformation was against this association. Even the involvement of the mother of Jesus in the visit to the grave was rejected.

The resurrection was separated from the experience of the women and became weightless. The various reports of the anxiety and comradeship of the women, which still took up a good deal of space in the New Testament, were put in the shade by the overwhelming light of the resurrection. The resurrection became earthless, the shadow story uninteresting. The victory was only seen in the light.

In the New Testament, the earthly side of the resurrection of Jesus is the story of the women on Easter morning. Despite all the patriarchal limitations imposed on it it was the basic material of the Easter experience, even if there were different versions of the narrative. According to the accounts, several women came to the tomb in the morning with oil and preparations for the body of Jesus; to their terror they discovered that the tomb was empty and heard the message that Jesus was risen. There are differences between the accounts after this: in Mark anxiety and dismay dominate the scene and the experiences of the women are portrayed with no ray of light. They experience the terror of the cross by the graveside: the end of the original conclusion to Mark (16.8) is panic, ecstasy and the flight of the women. Matthew already failed to perceive the unrelieved terror. He wanted the women also to rejoice.

For him 'great joy' has taken the place of fright (28.8). Least emotion can be detected in Luke: the women are afraid, but then they react quickly to the report that Jesus is risen. Although in his Gospel they are not given any special commission to proclaim - which is still the case in Mark and Mathew – they are good communicators and proclaim the resurrection to the disciples without any special commission.

The composition of the group also varies: in Mark four women seem to be witnesses of the death and resurrection (corresponding to the four disciples at the beginning of the Gospel: Peter, Andrew, James and John, Mark 1.16-19); they are Mary Magdalene, Mary the mother of James, Salome and the mother of Joses. The latter is mentioned only in connection with the death and burial. However, three women are distinctively present at the resurrection: Mary Magdalene, who has a special encounter with the risen Jesus (Mark 16.9ff.; John 20.1ff.), and two mothers who were known in the community for their famous sons. One of them is Salome, presumably the mother of the sons of Zebedee, who in contrast to their mother fled at the arrest of Jesus. Matthew also adds another Mary, who must be one of the two mothers, to the famous Mary Magdalene. In these compositions the important feature seems to me to be that the message of the resurrection is not only attached to the apostle Mary Magdalene but originally included two mothers (Mark) and later one mother (Matthew). Women seem more strongly than we can detect today to have been bearers of tradition in the early cuhrch. The mothers, grandmothers and mothers-in-law of Peter, John, James and Timothy are mentioned. We know of the mothers of community leaders but not of fathers. Where fathers are mentioned, they have no function as disciples. The female genealogy was important for handing on the story of Jesus.

In John 'a new principle of ordering'[14] has been introduced into the composition and listing of the group of women: the mothers of Jesus' family are in first place and Mary comes at the end (19.25).

Luke, whose understanding of women and the church comes closest to ours, now changes the group: alongside Mary Magdalene the apostle and Mary the mother of the community he puts Joanna, the wife of the finance minister at the court of king Herod, and risks the scandal of making a prominent woman, albeit one separated from her husband, witness to the resurrection. Alongside a tradition of an apostle and a recognized mother he has seen the important missionary role of the independent woman for the attestation and communication of the gospel[15] and bound together three social forms of the female life.

The pagan prehistory

Despite differing numbers and concepts the group of women has entered the tradition as a group of three, above all in art after the ninth century.

Martin Hengel sees the New Testament number three as an adaptation to male history: 'This tendency towards a group of three recalls that group of three which forms the closest nucleus of the Twelve, Peter, James and John, and also the three pillars in the primitive community of Jerusalem: James the brother of the Lord, Cephas and John.' It is also possible that there is a thought of the requirements of evidence, which according to Deut.19.15 called for two or three people, though in Judaism no woman could be a witness.

Here there seems to me to be a failure to take into account the background of the group in the history of religion. Three women or a woman with three faces are the primal model of all associations of three. They appear in many cultures down to the Middle Ages in images from the Celtic or Germanic period. They derive from matriarchal conceptions and represent the goddess in a threefold manifestation, mostly as a maiden, mother and old woman.

According to Heide Göttner-Abendroth the world-view of the developed matriarchy is characterized by the fact that the three-storey cosmos is completely permeated by feminine forces. Above there dwells the clear, atmospheric, youthful goddess. In the centre, dominating land and sea, lives the women's goddess who with her erotic power makes fertile earth and water, animals and humans, and thus preserves life. In the underworld dwells the old goddess, the goddess of death, as an old woman who destroys all life in the abyss and makes it rise again from the depths. All three figures together form only one deity, so they can never be completely separated.[16] Without doubt the three biblical women still represent the aspects of life, earth and death in a threefold form.

In the Celtic sphere, in the Lower German area of the Roman Empire, in isolated instances as far as the south of Upper Germany and also in Gaul, at a later period (from the second century AD) we find three individual figures, the so-called matrons, on stone monuments.[17] In a somewhat Byzantine way they sit rather rigidly side by side; they have broad cloaks and the two outer ones wear bonnets, the sign of a married woman, though they could also be recollections of the disc of the moon. The middle, young one has her hair let down. On their laps they hold fruit or cornucopias. As the goddesses of life and fertility down to a late period they represent a widespread popular religion and piety.

If we compare the Celtic German cult of matrons with the mediaeval pictures of the three women under the cross and at the tomb, we can see a similarity. The bonnet has become a nimbus and the fruit and cornucopias are now vessels containing oil. The hair of the young one (Mary Magdalene) is often let down. The three Christian women take up a story and continue a story of women which was firmly rooted in the people.

This pre-Christian group of three is combined in the West with women saints imported by Christianity. Down to the present day in Stes-Maries-de-la-Mer in the French Camargue there is a celebration of the three Maries of the sea, a gipsy festival in which the three biblical women coincide with a cult of a local triadic goddess. The three Bavarian maidens, Barbara with the tower, Margaret with the snake and Catharine with the wheel also go back to such pagan forbears, perhaps to the three 'eternals', though these above all represent virginity and not different stages of life.[18]

Like the three goddesses, the three women of the New Testament represent life in community and different stages. Now they represent it in different social roles. And they represent it in a deeper, more reflective way than their forbears: in the face of emptiness, death and abandonment.

The so-called pagan prehistory contains the story of our three women. When we look at it again, the story of the three women by the tomb also takes on new vitality. In addition to the threefold witness at the cross, the burial and the grave (Hengel), it also shows us our three phases of life, youth, motherhood and old age, as processes which belong inseparably together, of whose rhythms we are no longer aware in our linear patriarchal patterns of life. It shows us the variety which makes up our life and the reality of human relationships. It shows us the earthly side of resurrection which – with our gaze fixed to the risen one who is lifted up from the earth – we have failed to see.

If the Anna Selbdritt has maintained something of the Sophia love of God, the three women preserve a non-hierarchical pattern of life in which each represents a form of wholeness, and produces differentiation not in subordination, but in the fullness of existence. The experience of God has taken a social form.

Mary and monolithic sisterhood

Traditionally, Mary the mother of Jesus is not one of the three women. According to the three Synoptic Gospels, which contain the most reliable version of the story, she was not at the crucifixion, burial or tomb. Only John has put her under the cross with the beloved disciple. Only mediaeval art has put her in the group of women.

According to the synoptic accounts she must have been very sceptical about her son. But just as the humanity of Jesus increasingly disappeared with the reshaping of the Gospels, so too did his critical mother. In Luke the one who in Mark still regarded her son as a 'drop-out' has already become the understanding Mother of God who tries to comprehend her disobedient son when he stays behind in the temple.[19]

But Luke narrates the story of the women in the framework of a church history in which the dice have already been cast in favour of the group of male disciples and against the serving women. His Gospel, which is apparently so well-disposed towards women, no longer has an equal partnership of women and men but incorporates the women into a church structure governed by men. He has provided other models for women alongside Mary, but the more the church kept to patriarchal structures and thought-patterns, the more strongly it was fixed on one type of woman. It forgot the other figures of women who over the course of time were continually excluded from or defamed in the great church, so that they became the sinner, like Mary Magdalene, or the housewife, like Martha. We may infer from the history of the tradition that in revolutionary developments, in free churches, in subversive trends, figures like Mary Magdalene and Martha became symbols of unconventional Christian life. This happened to Mary much less often. She was taken over by the mainstream church, had to embody in herself every imaginable dream of femininity, and was turned from a living, critical, angry unadapted mother into the symbol of femininity. In patriarchal Christianity she thus provided a secret model with which many people could identify and represented an emotional release from the strict image of God the Father; as the old earth mother she also effectively represented national and earthly interests, as she still does today. For depth psychology, the virgin mother is at present a primal image 'that can make us aware of the goal of becoming human in the whole human being who grows together out of the contradictions of feminine and masculine, unconscious and conscious, earthly and divine'.[20]

In feminist theology she becomes apparently the only model with which women can identify; she is again cultivated as the symbolic model of new femininity. 'The image of Mary "rising"' says something... even to Mary Daly.[21] For others Mary is the only reality in Christianity, the feminine principle, 'the reborn, age-old goddess'. Catherina Halkes also hopes that on the basis of the Bible and theology, but in a far more cosmic and all-embracing way - also with the help of the history of religions – we may discover a Mary who is a powerful, prophetic and critical figure.[22] For her Mary is a 'symbol', which is an 'expansion, enrichment and tempering of our reality, above all of our experience of faith'. Today we have a massive return of Mary in feminist garb: what does she bring us, and what does she take away? According to Christa Mulack it is psychologically important that 'humanity, like God, can only be revealed through the feminine principle, because it alone is in a position to reconcile opposites and represent totality'. With Mary, for her 'timelessness breaks into temporality, and that was always possible only through the feminine. Again like is allied with like, feminine *ruach* with the human feminine. That is the mystery of the virgin who goes through all religions as mother and beloved and celebrates her resurrection with Christianity.'[23] A religious feminist understanding of revelation is developing which takes up Catholic conceptions of an ongoing revelation. Thus Catharina Halkes hopes that 'we shall hear from feminist theology the protest against the church's teaching that God's revelation has become final and therefore also complete with the life, death and resurrection of Jesus...' This ongoing incarnation of God happens among the oppressed women who 'take on a voice and a face'.[24] Mary Daly's second coming of God in women is the most extreme expression of these feminine hopes of revelation.[25]

Such feminist religion raises the question whether the hopes, the expectations which are set on such a symbol do not again in principle raise moral claims. The revelation of divinity and female principle in Mary and the discovery of women as divine media of revelation seem to me often to be bound up with stereotyped conceptions of 'femininity', with a picture of virgin woman which has no counterpart other than the Son, and shows ideology and intolerance towards other images.

The Canadian psychoanalyst Naomi Goldenberg has drawn attention to the relationships between 'one myth', 'one symbol' and 'one ethic':

> One ethic, one symbol and indeed one 'feminine principle' can only exist if all females agree about the significance of the symbol chosen or if all those who do not agree are considered deficient in regard to their femininity. It is probable that finding any simple image which reflects all the important values of all females is impossible. The desire of feminists to endorse any one image of 'proper' femininity could be a desire to stereotype women in a new role and to limit their possibilities within sisterhood.[26]

Here Naomi Goldenberg points to the absolutist elements e.g in Mary Daly's conceptions of sisterhood, to the feminist utopia which transcends our concrete social and personal conflict, in which there is joy, dance and laughter but no darkness, no evil and no depression, because these are caused by patriarchy: 'There is a tonality to Daly's work which denies plurality'.[27]

Mary as a women's symbol depicting fertility, the norm of a new women's culture and a monolithic sisterliness derived from her without wrinkles or flecks – as is dreamed of by some women in feminist theology – will never become a model for all women. Nor will she be able to become a model for a women's culture which is constantly developing and not stagnating. Byzantine rigidity in wishes and ideologies is already reflected in a symbolic figure.

We should ask today whether a feminist theology which

could give a liberating stamp to a post-patriarchal culture that on the one side has rediscovered the Catholic culture of images and myths could on the other also become aware of Protestant culture: the matriarchal principle of being accepted which embraces our whole reality does not need any revelations to take it further nor any divine heightening of our reality. From it comes the freedom of our person and our action and the priesthood of all believers, which in principle is not fixed to either sex.

The expectation of a new society of women and men is the expectation of many human models. This requires of a non-patriarchal Christianity radical openness for relationships of all kinds. As its standard and still unexhausted model we are offered the stories about Jesus with their relationships with women, with their failure and success, with death and resurrection. In these relationships Mary of Nazareth also has her place – as our sister.

One feminist principle, one Mary, one ethics, one faith – that is the patriarchal church in reverse. Our openness towards women and for the future are reproduced more truly and in a more pluralistic way by the three women of the early biblical tradition. They represent conflicts, otherness, sisterly dispute, friendship and community. They are harder to use and misuse (Mary has already been involved in too many things, which makes us sceptical). They form a unity in difference. Their image arose out of our own history and corresponds to our innermost interests.

Conclusion: The Bible and the Holy Spirit

Today we need a multiplicity of images and stories, for only in this way can we begin on and carry through the multiplicity of plans made by women. Only in this way can we remain open to what is developing in and among women. Only in this way can we be preserved from carrying on abstract female ideals, failing to see the reality of women and setting up methodical instructions for salvation.

We can hardly restore to life the mediaeval Annes and other saints, but we should track down the images of women in the Bible which correspond to our reality and our interests and bring them to the centre. This can happen in various ways: through reinterpretation e.g. of the Lucan Martha by the Johannine Martha;[28] through shadowy figures like Hagar which reproduce our own shadow (Gen.21.9ff.); through provocative and scandalous figures like Rahab, behind whom a priestess appears instead of the 'harlot' (Josh.2.1ff.; 6.17,25): through provocative political figures like Judith, who as the divine heroine did not correspond with any feminine ideal and who with her victory over Holofernes could replace the story of David and Goliath.[29] Through figures of contrast like Vashti, the first wife of king Ahasuerus, who rejected men, was replaced by Esther, disappeared from view in the Bible and must be recovered through our own history (Esther 1.9ff). And finally also through a venture into mythology. Lilith, the mythological first wife of Adam, who did not want to lie under him and was sent into the wilderness, no longer has a biblical background, but women oppressed by Eve's burden of guilt seek and need such a counterpart.[30]

Can the reform of iconography change tradition? Can new images brought into the centre change the general patriarchal denomination of Christianity? Naomi Goldenberg, who has raised this question, has also cautiously answered it in the affirmative and referred to the many new interpretations of traditional conceptions which were hostile to women in feminist theological literature, which show that the fate of women and the protest of women are attempts at an independent existence. In the Jewish-Christian tradition there are alternative images of women from which a new tradition can grow.[31]

But women must ask themselves today: is that not heresy? A deviation from the basic Christian and biblical position?

Many mediaeval images of women confirm that departures from the tradition were customary. Only with growing dogmatizing, increasing fear of heresy and the desire to secure oneself with a pure doctrine which corresponded to a sexually pure ideal of women were such independent drives cut off.

Regrettably, with the Reformation the imaginative and varied world of images was destroyed. Yet a new opportunity arose: the Bible became the people's book, could be read by all, and women began to discover themselves and the falsified interpretations in it. So Mary Magdalene was again accessible undisguised, became a new guideline for women and, as the church of modern times gained its independence, became the model of the eloquent, preaching woman. While the Reformers still had other favourite images of housewives like Sarah and Rebecca, and this remained the dominant picture in the mainstream Protestant churches, there were new developments on the sidelines. As early as 1650 the Quaker George Fox attempted a reform of iconography: he wanted to replace the old Eve-Mary typology with a new Eve-Magdalene typology, because the first witness to the resurrection and preacher of it seemed to him to be a more appropriate Christian image of women than Mary.[32]

But she was still within the framework of the Bible. Can we reject the patriarchal conception of women in the Bible and at the same time use non-biblical ('pagan', 'legendary conceptions')?[33] The position of the Bible in feminist theology is in fact a critical point. However, if we apply the Reformers' standard to it, whether 'they (the books) are about Christ',[34] we get a criterion. For many people today who have discovered Jesus through liberation theology, that means whether they are about the one who preaches deliverance to the captives and freedom to the oppressed (Luke 4.18), whether they help in the liberation of human beings for their human worth, advance their status as children of God. On the basis of his criterion Luther could call James a 'strawy epistle', because it taught justification by works instead of justification by faith.

Women today have the right, on the basis of this criterion, to reject passages which are hostile to women or reinterpret them because they violate their status as children of God.

In addition, something else becomes important for us: today we need dreams and fantasies, we need to find images and conceptions which help towards our healing. It is legitimate to take over Lilith, who arises out of the Bible, as a human possibility; this has the legitimation of the Holy Spirit who alongside scripture leads us to truth, makes us true. We must reflect on what Holy Spirit, who was originally feminine, means within a feminist theology and how she – the Spirit – changes us and the often distorted view of the Holy Spirit as a male figure. What consequences we draw from this for images of God we must leave to the free sphere of love, imagination and individual experience. The father image is not oppressive for all those who object to images which are hostile to women. However, for others the formula 'In the name of the Father, the Son and the Holy Spirit' demonstrates concealed male power. If we open up this imagery so that one day it can be filled anew with the Abba-Jesus relationship it will lose something of its force. In that case it will no longer have connotations of despotic power and blind obedience but will be filled with images of a deeply human character, of loneliness and not being forsaken, of grief and trust, without giving up the riddle of human existence. However, this seems to me to be hardly possible without the help of women's stories, women's images.

Both the iconoclasm as practised by some women today, and the prohibition of images as was disastrously practised in churches in the past, are wrong. Something new must grow in us and among us. Then what is old will fall away, die out of its own accord because it is rotten. It will be more difficult to let that happen than to call for radical solutions. Vashti and Esther, Lilith and Eve, the figures of contrast who are said to divide us from one another, must become sisters, tolerate conflicts, establish living relationships.

It is still an open question how and when we shall change theology, the church and even society by doing this. We have the images in us, in our bodies, in our self-consciousness. We develop them among us. They work from the inside outwards and vice versa. We are the church, and if we reject the pernicious heresy of the separation of spirit and body – which Philip Potter claims to be worse than all other heresies – we shall be in the thick of this process which cannot be restrained any longer. The old wayfarer's slogan with its closeness to the earth has again emerged as a watchword for our way: the land flowing with milk and honey.

NOTES

Introduction

1. Christa Wolf, *Voraussetzungen einer Erzählung: Kassandra*, Darmstadt 1983, 57.

2. J.J.Bachofen, *Das Mutterrecht*, Frankfurt 1975, 86; Erich Neumann, *Die grosse Mutter*, Olten 1956, 248ff.

3. Erich Fromm, *The Art of Loving*, Harper and Row 1974 and Allen and Unwin 1975, 46.61.

4. *TDOT* 3, 130f., s.v. *dbš*.

5. Heinrich Gross, *Die Idee des ewigen und allgemeinen Weltfriedens im alten Orient und im alten Testament*, Trier 1956, 74.

6. Horst Eberhard Richter, *Der Gotteskomplex*, Reinbek 1979, 99.

7. Jean Baker Miller, *Toward a New Psychology of Women*, Beacon Press, Boston 1976.

8. Adolf Schlatter, *Die christliche Ethik*, Calw 1914, 345.

9. Virginia Woolf, *A Room of One's Own* (1929), reissued Chatto and Windus/The Hogarth Press 1984, 106.

1. Autonomy

1. Carol Gilligan, *In a Different Voice*, Harvard University Press 1982, 173; Jean Baker Miller, op.cit., 83.

2. Evelyne Sullerot, *Die Wirklichkeit der Frau*, Munich 1979, 348ff.

3. Mariama Bâ, *Ein so langer Brief*, Zug 1980, 85.

4. Betty Friedan, *The Second Stage*, Summit Books 1981.

5. Maxie Wander, *Guten Morgen, du Schöne*, Darmstadt 1978, 32.

6. Helene Simon, *Elisabeth Gnauck-Kühne, Eine Pilgerfahrt*, Mönchen-Gladbach 1928.

7. *Berliner Beitrag zur Studie des ÖRK 'Männer und Frauen in der Kirche'*, 5.

8. Margarete Mitscherlich, 'Im Gefängnis der eigenen Psyche', *Emma* 5, 1978, 18f.

9. Marlis Gerhardt, in *Die Überwindung der Sprachlosigkeit*, ed. G.Dietze, Darmstadt 1978, 26.
10. Marina Möller-Gambaroff, 'Emanzipation macht Angst', in *Kursbuch* 47, 23.
11. *Emma* 10, 1981, 38.

2. What is Patriarchy?

1. Marina Möller-Gambaroff, 'Emanzipation macht Angst', 18.
2. Erich Neumann, *Die grosse Mutter*, 67.
3. Kate Millett, *Sexual Politics*, Doubleday, New York 1969, 25.
4. Mary Daly, *Beyond God the Father*, Beacon Press, Boston 1973, 13f.
5. Ernest Borneman, *Das Patriarchat*, Frankfurt 1975, 104f., 542.
6. Marie-Luise Janssen-Jurreit, *Sexismus*, Munich 1976, 712.
7. Johann Jakob Bachofen, *Das Mutterrecht*, Frankfurt 1975.
8. E.g. Robert Briffault, *The Mothers* (1929), Johnson Reprint Corporation, New York 1977; Robert Graves, *The White Goddess*, Octagon Books, New York 1982.
9. Jürgen Moltmann. 'Ich glaube an Gott den Vater', *Evangelische Theologie* 43.5, 297ff.
10. G.Kaper et al., *Eva, wo bist du?*, Gelnhausen 1981, 15f.
11. Karl Barth, *Church Dogmatics* I, 2, T.& T.Clark 1956, 193, 195.
12. Elisabeth Moltmann-Wendel, 'Partnerschaft', in *Frauen auf neuen Wegen*, ed. C.Pini et al., Gelnhausen 1978, 271ff.
13. Hanna Wolff, *Jesus der Mann*, Stuttgart 1975.
14. E.g. Christa Mulack, *Die Weiblichkeit Gottes*, Stuttgart 1983.
15. W.A.Visser 't Hooft, *Gottes Vaterschaft im Zeitalter der Emancipation*, Frankfurt 1982.
16. Philip Potter, 'Partnerschaft aus einem neuen Verstehen der Bibel', in *Mitteilungen* (Badene Landeskirche), October 1981, 10, 40.
17. Horst Eberhart Richter, *Der Gotteskomplex*, Reinbek 1979, 98ff.
18. Etty Hillesum, *Etty: A Diary 1941-1943*, Granada Publishing 1985 (US Title: *An Interrrupted Life. The Diaries of Etty Hillesum*, New York 1983), 232.

NOTES

3. The Forgotten Goddess

1. Virginia Woolf, *A Room of One's Own*, 43.
2. Mary Daly, *Gyn/ecology*, Beacon Press, Boston 1978 and The Women's Press 1979, 178.
3. J.J.Bachofen, *Das Mutterrecht*, 1.
4. Sir Galahad, *Mütter und Amazonen*, Frankfurt 1981, 30.
5. J.J.Bachofen, *Das Mutterrecht*, 12f., 20.
6. Sir Galahad, op.cit., 28.
7. Josefine Schreier, *Göttinnen*, Munich 1977.
8. Ernest Borneman, *Das Patriarchat*, 82.
9. Marie E.P.Konig, 'Die Frau im Kult der Eiszeit', in R.Fester et al., *Weib und Macht*, Frankfurt 1980, 107ff.
10. Richard Fester, 'Das Protokoll der Sprache', in R.Fester et al, *Weib und Macht*, 79ff.
11. Heide Göttner-Abendroth, *Die Göttin und ihr Heros*, Munich 1980, 22. Cf. also Robert Graves, *The White Goddess*.
12. Cf. Ernest Borneman, op.cit., 123.
13. Uwe Wesel, *Der Mythos vom Matriarchat*, Frankfurt 1980, 52.
14. Ibid., 106.
15. Sally R.Binford, 'Are Goddesses and Matriarchies Merely Figments of Feminist Imagination?', in *The Politics of Women's Spirituality*, ed. C.Spretnak, New York 1982. Cf. also Beate Wanger, *Zwischen Mythos und Realität*, Frankfurt 1982.
16. Marie-Luise Janssen-Jurreit, op.cit., 148.
17. Adrienne Rich, 'Prepatriarchal Female/Goddess Images', in *The Politics of Women's Spirituality*, 33.
18. Starhawk, 'Witchcraft as Goddess Religion', in *The Politics of Women's Spirituality*, New York 1982, 51.
19. Judith Ochshorn, *The Female Experience and the Nature of the Divine*, Bloomington 1982, 131f.
20. Heide Göttner-Abendroth, op.cit., 32.
21. Adrienne Rich, op.cit., 34.
22. Jean Baker Miller, *Identitätsbewusstsein bei Frau und Mann und die Schlüsselprobleme unserer Zeit*, Doc. DUMC 14, WCC.
23. Christa Wolf, *Voraussetzungen einer Erzählung: Kassandra*, 57.

4. Feminist Theology

1. Cf. above all the basic introduction, Catharina Halkes, *Gott hat nicht nur starke Söhne*, Gütersloh 1980; Elisabeth Schüssler-Fiorenza, 'Breaking the Silence – Becoming Visible', *Concilium* 182, 1985, 3ff.

NOTES

2. *Epd.Dokumentation* 1978, no.25.

3. James H.Cone, *Black Theology and Black Power*, Seabury Press, New York 1969; Gustavo Gutierrez, *Theology of Liberation*, Orbis Books, Maryknoll and SCM Press 1974.

4. Cf. Jutta Menschik, *Feminismus. Geschichte, Theorie, Praxis*, Cologne 1977; Herrad Schenk, *Die feministische Herausförderung*, Munich 1980.

5. For feminist methodology cf. Renate Duelli-Klein et al., *Feministische Wissenschaft und Frauenstudium*, Hamburg 1982.

6. Katharina Rutschky, *Schwarze Pädagogik*, Frankfurt 1977.

5. The Bible and Feminine Self-awareness

1. Margaret Mead, *Male and Female*, Gollancz 1950.

2. August Bebel, *Die Frau und der Sozialismus*, Berlin 1973, 84.

3. Simone de Beauvoir, *The Second Sex* (1949), Penguin Books 1972, 128f.

4. Elizabeth Gould Davis, *The First Sex*, Penguin Books 1975.

5. Ute Gerhard et al. (eds.), *Dem Reich der Freiheit werb'ich Bürgerinnen. Die Frauenzeitung von Louise Otto*, Frankfurt 1980, 37.

6. Helene Lange, *Lebenserinnerungen*, Berlin 1925, 271f.

7. G.W. and L.A.Johnson (eds.), *Josephine Butler*, J.W.Arrowsmith 1929, 66.

8. Hanna Wolff, *Jesus als Psychotherapeut*, Stuttgart 1978, 137.

9. Elisabeth Moltmann-Wendel, *The Women around Jesus*, SCM Press and Crossroad Publishing Company, New York 1982, 119, 131.

10. Leonard Swidler, 'Jesu Begegnung mit Frauen: Jesus als Feminist', E.Moltmann (ed.), *Menschenrechte fur die Frau*, Munich 1974, 130ff.

11. Hanna Wolff, *Jesus der Mann*, 80.

12. Leonard Swidler, 'Jesu Begegnung mit Frauen', 130f.

13. Elisabeth Schüssler-Fiorenza, 'Die Rolle der Frau in der urchristlichen Bewegung', *Concilium* 12.1, 1976, 7 (in this period not all issues of *Concilium* were translated into English).

14. Elisabeth Schüssler-Fiorenza, 'The Twelve', in L. and A.Swidler (ed.), *Women Priests*, New York 1977, 118ff.

15. Hartwig Thyen, '...nicht mehr männlich und weiblich', in Crüsemann and Thyen, *Als Mann und Frau geschaffen*, Gelnhausen 1978, 186ff.

16. Cf.also Klaus Thraede, 'Ärger mit der Freiheit', in Scharffenorth and Thraede, *Freunde in Christus werden*, Gelnhausen 1977, 112ff.

17. Elisabeth Moltmann-Wendel, *The Women around Jesus*, 61ff.
18. Karl Künstle, *Ikonografie der christlichen Kunst*, Freiburg 1926, 2, 427.
19. *Corpus Christianorum* 36, 18, 23-6.
20. Cf. Karl E.Børresen, 'Die anthropologischen Grundlagen der Beziehungen zwischen Mann und Frau in der klassischen Theologie', *Concilium* 12.1, 1976, 11f.
21. Adolf Brandmeyer (ed.), *Kirchliche Verkündigung unter Frauen*, Gütersloh 1940, 48.
22. Adolf Schlatter, *Die christliche Ethik*, 155.
23. *The Jerome Biblical Commentary*, Geoffrey Chapman 1968, II, 330.
24. *A New Catholic Commentary on Holy Scripture*, Nelson 1969, 1141.
25. Elisabeth Schüssler-Fiorenza, 'Die Rolle der Frau', 7.
26. Bernadette Brooten, 'Junia... Outstanding among the Apostles', in *Women Priests*, ed. L.A.Swidler, Paulist Press, New York 1979, 141ff.

6. God, our Mother

1. Irene von Bourbon Parma, *Concilium* 143, 1983, 113f., 119.
2. Catharina Halkes, ibid., 104.
3. In E.Moltmann Wendel, *Frau und Religion. Gotteserfahrungen im Patriarchat*, Frankfurt 1983, 194.
4. Ibid., 201.
5. Christa Mulack, *Die Weiblichkeit Gottes*, 9ff.
6. Mary Daly, *Beyond God the Father*, 82ff.
7. Heide Göttner-Abendroth, *Die Göttin und ihr Heros*, 8.
8. Ursa Krattiger, *Die perlmutterne Mönchin*, Stuttgart 1983, 119f.
9. H.Denziger, *Enchiridion Symbolorum*, Freiburg 1947, 127.
10. Elisabeth Schüssler-Fiorenza, *In Memory of Her*, Crossroad Publishing Company, New York and SCM Press 1983, 130ff.; Urs Winter, *Frau und Göttin*, Gottingen 1983.
11. Felix Christ, *Jesus Sophia*, Zurich 1970.
12. Rosemary Ruether, 'The Female Nature of God: A Problem in Contemporary Religious Life', *Concilium* 143, 1981, 62f.
13. Cf. Yves Congar, *I Believe in the Holy Spirit*, Geoffrey Chapman 1983; Andrew Greeley, *The Mary Myth: On the Femininity of God*, Seabury Press, New York 1977; L.Swidler, *Biblical Affirmations of Women*, Philadelphia 1979.
14. Jürgen Moltmann, 'Die Gemeinschaft des Heiligen Geistes', *Theologische Literaturzeitung* 107, 1982, 711.

15. Hahn and Reichel (eds.), *Zinzendorf und Herrnhuter Brüder*, Hamburg 1977, 293.

16. Joachim Jeremias, *The Prayers of Jesus*, SCM Press and Fortress Press, Philadelphia 1967, 62.

17. Christa Mulack, op.cit., 333.

18. Gerhard Lohfink, *Jesus and Community*, Fortress Press, Philadelphia and SPCK 1985, 45f.

7. *Matriarchal Sub-culture*

1. Leonard Swidler, *Biblical Affirmations of Women*, 22f.; cf. Marija Gimbutas, *The Gods and Goddesses of Old Europe*, University of California Press 1974, 238; cf. Merlin Stone, *When God was a Woman*, Dial Press, New York 1976, 179.

2. Heide Göttner-Abendroth, *Die Göttin und ihr Heros*, 174.

3. Ernst Bloch, *Atheismus im Christentum*, Frankfurt 1968, 102.

4. Margarita Woloschin, *Die grüne Schlange*, Frankfurt 1982, 208f.

5. Helgard Balz-Cochois, *Gomer. Der Höhenkult Israels im Selbstverständnis der Volksfrömmigkeit*, Frankfurt 1982, 194.

6. Ingrid Schlicther, 'Frauenoffensive', *Journal* no.9, Munich 1978, 52.

7. Hans Egli, *Das Schlangensymbol*, Olten 1983; Uwe Steffen, *Drachenkampf*, Stuttgart 1984.

8. Gertrud Schiller, *Ikonographie der christlichen Kunst*, Gütersloh 1971, Vol.3, 32.

9. Erich Neumann, 'Die Bedeutung des Erdarchetyps für die Neuzeit', in *Eranos Jahrbuch* 1953.

10. Ingeborg Tetzlaff, *Romanische Kapitelle in Frankreich*, Cologne 1979, 133f.

11. Gertrud Schiller, *Ikonografie der christlichen Kunst*, Vol.2, 121, 426.

12. Elisabeth Moltmann-Wendel, *The Women around Jesus*, 39ff.; ead., 'Die domestizierte Martha', *Evangelische Theologie* 24, 1982, 1, 26.

13. Ernst Bloch, *Atheismus im Christentum*, 232.

14. Ernst Harnischfeger, *Mystik im Barock*, Stuttgart 1980, 106.

NOTES

8. The Women's Jesus

1. Mary Daly, *Beyond God the Father*, 69.

2. Rosemary Ruether, *Sexism and God Talk*, Beacon Press, Boston and SCM Press 1983, 122ff.

3, W.A.Visser 't Hooft, *Gottes Vaterschaft im Zeitalter der Emanzipationen*, 188.

4. For this and what follows, Ruether, op.cit., 127ff.

5. Elaine Pagels, *The Gnostic Gospels*, Random House, New York and Weidenfeld and Nicholson 1980, 94ff.

6. Epiphanius, Panarion, in *A New Eusebius*, ed. J.Stevenson, SPCK 1957, 113.

7. Julian of Norwich, *Revelations of Divine Love*, Penguin Books 1966, ch.64, p.176.

8. Hanna Wolff, *Jesus der Mann*, 80.

9. Christa Mulack, *Die Weiblichkeit Gottes*, 287.

10. Heide Göttner-Abendroth, *Die Göttin und ihr Heros*, 127.

11. Felix Christ, *Jesus Sophia*, 154.

12., Gertrud Schiller, *Ikonografie der christlichen Kunst*, 2, 360 plate 142.

13. Ibid., 366 plate 156.

14. Anton Mayer, *Der zensierte Jesus*, Olten 1983, 94.

15. Luise Schottroff, 'Maria Magdalena und die Frauen am Grabe Jesu', *Evangelische Theologie* 42.1, 12.

16. Elisabeth Schüssler-Fiorenza, *In Memory of Her*, 320.

17. Carol Gilligan, *In a Different Voice*, 62.

18. Erika Schuchardt, *Warum gerade ich...? Behinderung und Glaube*, Gelnhausen 1981, 104.

19. Elisabeth Moltmann-Wendel, *The Women around Jesus*, 30.

20. Ibid., 39ff.

21. Schiller, *Ikonografie der christlichen Kunst* 1, pl.427. Cf. also 3, pl.71.

22. Ibid., 3, 35.

23. Ibid., 39 n.20.

9. Mutuality

1. Isabel Carter Heyward, *The Redemption of God. A Theology of Mutual Relation*, Washington 1982.

2. Beverly Wildung Harrison, 'The Power of Anger in the Work of Love', *Union Seminary Quarterly Review* XXXVI, 1981, 41-57.

3. Rosemary R.Ruether, *Sexism and God Talk*, 138.

4. Helm Stierlin, *Das Tun des Einen ist das Tun des Andern*, Frankfurt 1971, 66ff.

5. Elisabeth Moltmann-Wendel, *The Women around Jesus*, 30.

6. G.Kaper et al., *Eva, wo bist du?*, 15f.

7. Horst Eberhard Richter, *Lernziel Solidarität*, Reinbek 1974, 53.

10. Self-love

1.Erich Fromm, *The Art of Loving*, 59.

2. Paul Tillich, *The Shaking of the Foundations*, Penguin Books 1962, 155ff.

3. Manfred Haustein, 'Annahme in der therapeutischen Seelsorge und biblisch-reformatorischen Rechtfertigungslehre', in *Zeichen der Zeit* 37, Nov 1983, 277.

4. ...*opera nos non faciunt bonos, sed bonitas nostra, immo bonitas Dei facit nos bonos et opera nostra bona*, Johannes Ficker (ed.), *Luthers Vorlesungen über den Römerbrief 1515-1516*, Leipzig 1908, 221.

5. Alice Walker, *The Colour Purple*, Harcourt, Brace Jovanovich, New York and The Women's Press, 1983, 165. Used by permission.

6. *Non enim justa operando, justi efficimur, sed justi essendi justa operamur*, Ficker, op.cit., 91.

7. *Korrespondenz die Frau*, 11, 1981, 7.

8. Luise Rinser, *Den Wolf umarmen*, Frankfurt 1981, 162.

9. Judith Plaskow, *Sex, Sin and Grace*, University Press of America, Washington 1980, 157.

10. E.Moltmann-Wendel, 'Frau und Religion. Gotteserfahrungen im Patriarchat', 31ff.

11. Marianne Schuller, ' "Weibliche Neurose" und Identität', in Kamper Wulf (ed.), *Die Wiederkehr des Körpers*, Frankfurt 1982, 190.

12. Christa Wolf in Maxie Wander, *Guten Morgen, du Schöne*, Darmstadt 1978, 15.

13. Alice Walker, *The Colour Purple*, 167.

14. Martin Luther, *Ausgewählte Werke*, Munich 1938, I ,145.

15.Jean Baker Miller, *Identitätsbewusstsein bei Frau und Mann und die Schlüsselprobleme unserer Zeit*, Doc.CWMC 14 of WCC preparatory paper for the women's consultation in Sheffield, 1981.

16. Valerie Saiving Goldstein, 'The Human Situation: A Feminine Viewpoint', in *The Nature of Man*, ed. Simon Doniger, Harper and Bros, New York 1962, 153.

NOTES

11. Patriarchal and Matriarchal Love

1. See E.Schüssler-Fiorenza, *In Memory of Her*, 130ff.
2. Julius Schniewind, *Das Evangelium nach Matthäus*, Göttingen 1950, 71.
3. Anders Nygren, *Agape and Eros*, SPCK 1953, 48.
4. *TDNT* 1, 36 n.80.
5. Ibid., 37f..
6. Ibid., 36 n.80.
7. J.J Bachotten, *Das Mutterrecht*, 12f.
8. Erich Fromm, *The Art of Loving*, 45f.
9. Ernst Troeltsch, *The Social Teaching of the Christian Churches*, Allen and Unwin and Macmillan, New York 1931, 81.
10. Nygren, op.cit., 109ff.
11. Carol Gilligan, *In a Different Voice*, 212.
12. Agnes Sapper, *Die Familie Pfäffling*, Stuttgart 1966.
13. Erich Fromm, *Art of Loving*, 58.
14. Valerie S.Goldstein, 'The Human Situation: A FeminineViewpoint', 153.

12. Models for Women

1. H.E.Richter, *Der Gotteskomplex*, 225.
2. Mary Daly, *Gyn/ecology*, 37f.
3. Marjorie Suchocki, 'The Unmale God, Reconsidering the Trinity', in *Quarterly Review* 3,1, Spring 1983, 48. Cf E.Drewermann et al., *Trinität*, Freiburg 1984.
4. Patricia Wilson Kastner, *Faith, Feminism and the Christ*, Philadelphia 1983, 127.
5. Margaret Farley, 'New Patterns of Relationship: Beginnings of a Moral Revolution', in Walter Burkhardt (ed.), *Woman, New Dimensions*, New York 1975, 51-70.
6. Uwe Gerber, 'Feministische Theologie', *Theologische Literaturzeitung* 8, August 1984.
7. Barbara Hilkert Andolsen, 'Agape in Feminist Ethics', *Journal of Religious Ethics* 9.1, Spring 1981, 80.
8. See Erich Neumann, *Die grosse Mutter*, 310.
9. See Beda Kleinschmidt, *Die Heilige Anna*, Düsseldorf 1930.
10. Ibid., 164.
11. Shulamith Shahar, *Die Frau im Mittelalter*, Frankfurt 1983, 105.
12. Kleinschmidt, op.cit., 25.
13. Schiller, *Ikonografie der christlichen Kunst* 3, 31.

14. Martin Hengel, 'Maria Magdalena und die Frauen als Zeugen' in *Abraham unser Vater*, Festschrift O.Michel, Tübingen 1963, 243ff.

15. See E.Moltmann-Wendel, *The Women around Jesus*, 140ff.

16. Heide Göttner-Abendroth, *Die Göttin und ihr Heros*, 17.

17. Günther Ristow, *Römischer Götterhimmel und frühes Christentum*, Cologne 1980, 42.

18. Erich Jung, *Germanische Götter und Helden*, Munich 1922, 177f.

19. Cf. E.Moltmann-Wendel, 'Motherhood or Friendship', *Concilium* 168. 1983, 18.

20. Maria Kassel, 'Mary and the Human Psyche considered in the Light of Depth Psychology', ibid., 80.

21. Mary Daly, *Beyond God the Father*, 89.

22. Catharina Halkes, *Gott hat nicht nur stärke Sohne*, Gütersloh 1980, 116.

23. Christa Mulack, *Die Weiblichkeit Gottes*, 180, 272.

24. Catharina Halkes, 'Feministische Theologie. Eine Zwischenbilanz', in Brooten and Greinacher (eds), *Frauen in der Männerkirche*, Mainz and Munich 1982, 167.

25. Mary Daly, *Beyond God the Father*, 95.

26. Naomi Goldenberg, *The End of God*, Ottawa 1982, 108.

27. Ibid., 111.

28. Elisabeth Moltmann-Wendel, *The Women around Jesus*, 25ff.

29. Cf. Hans Mayer, *Aussenseiter*, Frankfurt 1975, 38f.

30. Siegmund Hurwitz, *Lililth, Die Erste Eva*, Zurich 1980.

31. Naomi Goldenberg, op.cit., 91.

32. Elisabeth Moltmann-Wendel, 'Motherhood or Friendship', 21.

33. Peter Beyerhaus, *Frauen im theologischen Aufstand*, Stuttgart 1983; Ingeborg Hauschildt, *Gott eine Frau?*, Wuppertal 1983.

34. *WA Deutsche Bibel* 7, 384 lines 25ff.